MW00460195

THE MICRO-INFLUENCER'S
BRAND PARTNERSHIP BIBLE

ASHLEIGH WARREN

THE MICRO INFLUENCER'S
BRAND
PARTNERSHIP
BIBLE

GROW YOUR **INCOME**,
FOLLOWING & **BRAND**

LIONCREST
PUBLISHING

COPYRIGHT © 2022 ASHLEIGH WARREN
All rights reserved.

THE MICRO-INFLUENCER'S BRAND PARTNERSHIP BIBLE
Grow Your Income, Following & Brand

FIRST EDITION

ISBN   978-1-5445-3116-8 *Hardcover*
       978-1-5445-3117-5 *Paperback*
       978-1-5445-3118-2 *Ebook*

CONTENTS

INTRODUCTION

You, a screen, and Google. That is how it is most days, for most influencers, when they're starting out. So first and foremost, and before we get tactical—and I teach you all the strategies you need to know to grow your income, following, and brand—I have to say this:

NEVER FORSAKE SMALL BEGINNINGS

The little wins that only you know about matter. Celebrating your first five hundred followers is important. Or, those eight people who commented on the post you thought was risky. Or when the brand you tagged acknowledged you back. Appreciating the small wins is the practice that separates the influencers who stick with it and succeed from the ones who don't. The strategic, foundational stuff you need to build a sustainable brand and business I can teach you. That's why I wrote this book. But, the practice of appreciating the journey, no one can teach you that but you. And it's so, so important because the journey to influencer success involves learning *a freaking lot*.

To truly build a successful, sustainable business and career, you have to master the roles of all the people you would find at a traditional marketing agency. *You* have to be the branding expert, digital marketer, creative director, photographer, videographer, TV host, copywriter, lawyer, agent, and more. And there are so many questions to answer at every step.

First, you have to nail your niche, brand vibe, and image. *How do I express myself better online? Did I choose the right niche? What do I choose for a color palette?* Then, what you choose dictates who your audience will be and what resonates with them. *Am I targeting the right audience? Is this new content I'm trying shit? Why aren't they commenting?* Once you crack the code, you then have to figure out how to get paid. *How do I pitch myself to brands? How much do I charge? How do I make an actual career out of this?* Not to mention there's so much to know once you get a deal, like contracts and legal concepts.

With so many aspects to consider, it's much easier to question what you're doing all the time than to not. There is just so much bad information out there too. It's easy to have moments where you scroll through your phone, see the mega influencers you look up to who are crushing it, and think, *I can never get there.* But any influencer who has "made it" started wherever you are today. Success as an influencer is a replicable formula.

I know that because it's what I do. The only difference between them and you is they have learned the most effective strategies. So anytime you get caught up thinking you can't, come back to this intro, read this, and sit with it: *You can.* Everyone starts somewhere.

THE MASSIVE MONEYMAKING OPPORTUNITY AHEAD OF YOU AND WHY I KNOW YOU CAN WIN

I'm not going to pretend I know where you're at in life right now. But my guess is, you're here because you want more. And, getting to that *more* for you at this moment involves being strategic around your influencer career. That might be because it's a potential avenue you want to explore. Maybe you're already in and committed. You might have four thousand followers, or only four hundred, and you want to keep growing. I promise you that if you use the strategies here, they will get you there wherever your version of there is. With persistence and by applying the right techniques, you can make any vision you want a reality.

Not long ago, I was in a similar place. I had just finished college and was working at Starbucks making twelve dollars an hour while trying to figure it out. My life was good but I had one recurring thought: *Is this it?* I was thirsty for more. Like, *What am I really here to do?* Then, I'd be on break during a shift scrolling through my phone and think, *Dang, I could make more money working for myself from my phone!* Back then, it seemed possible but also pretty far out of my reach. I definitely didn't know then what I know now, that success online is a formula. So I am grateful to be in a position to write this book and share that knowledge with you.

Like you, I saw an opportunity. I like to think that had I found a book like this that time, it probably would have changed my life way faster. I can't tell you how many nights I was up until 2:00 a.m. trying to figure out how to become the marketer I wanted to be. Now I work with the world's top influencers. Looking back, all I can say is, hard work pays off.

We may not know each other yet, but I think you are very smart to be investing time to learn and grow your influencer career. It is by far one of the smartest career options today. Influencers check the boxes on the four criteria most people want in a vocation these days. You can:

☐ Do what you love
☐ Have complete control over your time
☐ Serve a community you care about
☐ Make money from your phone

I give you props for being a smart-as-f*ck human who wants to cash in on your opportunity to run your own operation, control what you make, manage your time, and direct how you use your talents. Social media has made it easy for *anyone* (like you) to make a living sharing about *whatever* they care about from their kitchen island, wearing pajamas...or from the sand of Venice Beach...or an Airbnb treehouse in Bali.

Even if what you love is super niche or weird, you can probably make money from it. Maybe you're passionate about men's fashion and mental health. Cool. Or makeup is your thing. Awesome. Or, you're obsessed with the zero-waste lifestyle. That's amazing. A successful influencer business and the lifestyle that comes with it is possible for you—100 percent.

Plus, let's be honest, the work approach of earlier generations flat out does not make sense anymore. Your parents probably drove forty-five minutes in traffic to a concrete office block, sat in a soulless cubicle, and cranked out a nine-to-five workday in return for a sad bimonthly paycheck. Today, we have choices. #blessed. Most jobs can be done from anywhere you have an internet connection and in less than eight hours. Studies have shown that human productivity is capped at about five hours per day. So, of course, sponsored content ("sponcon") is now a viable business model and is growing. Ordinary people with engaged online communities are getting paid by brands—the Sephoras, Adidases, and Patagonias of the world—to promote their products. And you can easily be one of them.

Like most of the micro influencers I work with, you likely have an entrepreneurial spirit and creative mind. You probably also care about doing work that fulfills you and that offers you control and work-life balance. The only problem you might have is that you don't quite know how to maneuver that life. But all that is between you and a future where you're cashing checks from H&M is learning and applying a handful of strategies. To succeed, you have to become a skilled self-marketer, which this book will teach you. So here, you'll learn how to:

1. Refine your brand and content so it attracts the people you want in your community.
2. Engage intelligently with your audience and track your metrics.
3. Effectively pitch yourself to brands (big or small) who pay you well to share with your audience who pay you to post.

You will learn everything here and soon be laughing when you get DMs like these:

> Become a brand ambassador! Do a shit ton of work for free for $20 worth of product! K love you bye.

We'd love to offer you $50 to post 112 stories for our brand.

Hey, we like your vibe. Post pics of yourself wearing our clothes, and we'll send you a T-shirt you can keep.

Yeah, how about no? I am shaking my head as I write this. These messages are why I thoroughly enjoy helping micro influencers like you. I love when my inbox is flooded with wins instead. It would make my day to get a message from you soon that says:

I scored my first brand partnership deal!

I just got a check in the mail for $300 from an Instagram post!

I made $8,000/month this year and quit that job I hated.

I celebrate when I hear the success stories of influencers I work with every day—from the micro to the mega—who are crushing it. There are so many insanely talented creators being compensated for their creativity.

These days, instead of gaining exposure at the local open mic night, female comedians in their twenties make $6,000 per month posting pop-culture spoofs on Instagram and TikTok. Shout out to @sarahdaisyy, one creator I know who is crushing it. Content creators like @madcrayy get paid to take epic shots of themselves twirling in fields of flowers. Maddy was once a hobbyist photographer seeking creative escape from a dull nine-to-five and was so successful she had to say buh-bye to her boring job. The job title "menswear and lifestyle creator" is now a legit one too. Talented guys like

@stevensharpejr are earning serious coin by posting pics of themselves rocking sick leather jackets, helping the next generation look good.

As I write this book in late 2021, there are 37.8 million influencers, and that number is growing fast. In the last two years, brands have nearly doubled their spend on the creators they activate for advertising campaigns. Nowadays, it seems everybody wants to be an influencer. But, only a small fraction will be successful. It will be the people who understand that micro influencers hold all the power with large corporations and know how to wield it.

Massive global brands like Lululemon Athletica, Sephora, and Hilton Hotels & Resorts are looking to partner with creators like you at this very moment. So treat what you learn here as sacred. I called this book a bible for a reason. Put the strategies into play, and you *will* be successful.

I *know* you can win at this. I say that with total confidence because building talent-backed brands is a game I know how to play and continue to master.

THE SO SOCIAL BACKSTORY

My agency, So Social, dominates the marketing game for mega influencers and celebrities. We are the experts at finding new ways to grow their earnings and presence online. My team has worked our Instagram magic on major players in every industry, including Post Malone, MrBeast, Dude Perfect, Aaliyah, David Dobrik, Kesha, T-Pain, Markiplier, Jake Paul, Becca Kufrin, Try Guys, Sam & Colby, Addison Rae,

Pokimane, Shawn Mendes, King Bach, Steve Aoki, plus many more. We have had partnerships with major corporations like Fanjoy, LiveNation, Rivals, Island Records, and Empire Music. We are also liaisons with brands looking to outsource their content to micro influencers. We have serviced over 40,000 micro influencers to date, helping them create more effective strategies to grow and earn on social media's top platforms.

Often, our services are white-labeled to elite influencers by their internal management and marketing teams to help grow their exposure and sales on Instagram. Deadass, a lot of them don't even know we exist. And I love that. All they know is that they are making a ton of money each month and increasing their engagement on Instagram. My job is not to be famous but to make my clients look good and scale their presence and earnings.

Cold outreach is responsible for 90 percent of our client roster. We have over an 85 percent retention rate. We flat-out know how to speak to brands and influencers. We understand how to get them to work with us and earn them explosive results. Most of our success—about 80 percent—has come from follow-up and follow-through. There's a formula to generating wealth online, and it mostly comes from effectively defining and targeting your market.

Like you, I once aspired to build my own business so I could make my own hours and work from my laptop or cell phone from wherever I wanted: my sofa at home, poolside in Santorini, or a private airport on my way to an epic concert. My dream was also to build a remote lifestyle and do work I loved on *my terms*, because why would anyone want to live for the weekend, sit at a desk for eight hours a day from Monday to Friday, and make someone else rich?

Seven years ago as of this writing, I bet on myself. In 2014, I quit my full-time marketing job to start an agency. What drove me was an ache for freedom and a desire to never again be overworked for extremely little pay. That and the traditional, old ad agency model never really resonated. I wanted to build a business where marketing was treated as full-bodied. It is equal parts killer creative, voice, targeting and analytics. Traditional work models were never my thing. So I said eff all that. I got creative. I found my early clients on Craigslist and with Instagram hashtags. I did a shit ton of cold DM outreach and in no time began to crush it.

My first partnership was with a beauty client that made me over $700,000 in a little over a year. Yes, *one* client. In a short time, I was making over $30,000 per month consistently. Today, that number is way more because I was persistent and continued to learn and evolve as these billion-dollar platforms did and used the strategies that *work* (and that I teach in this book).

Our agency's success with mega influencers naturally led to an influx of DMs in my inbox from micro influencers. I'd get email requests that would say, "Hey, I would love your help with my influencer career, but I am not at the mega influencer level yet." Or, "How do I learn more?" Or, "How do I make money sharing products with my 1,000 followers?" Every time I get these kinds of messages, I ask myself: how do I serve the micro influencers who are passionate, hungry to learn, and such great people who genuinely want to make a positive impact in the world?

Micro influencers are in an entirely separate lane from the mega variety. They have a completely different roadmap for what they need to implement in order to expect and replicate continuous success. Most of them also don't have management or teams of photographers, videographers, editors, creative directors, or makeup artists—*yet*.

So in 2021, I launched Built to Influence, a community for micro influencers that offers them elite training and access to a team of VIP social marketing professionals, brand partnership databases, and over a thousand resources and templates for everything from winning at negotiations to pitching media outlets.

I love the work I do with micro influencers. You are such good-natured humans who are so passionate about so many topics. You have a thirst for growth. You genuinely want to learn and apply your new knowledge and make a positive impact. You want financial stability, a life-changing opportunity, and to make an impact in your communities and their families. Case in point: you are taking the time to read this book.

I get so much joy from working with influencers like you who have such a strong sense of community and hustle in them—often more than the mega influencers—because you need this to work. You are trying to earn more than a living, which makes me smile so hard—that is living! You are trying to bring like-minded people together and empower them to live better lives by teaching them what you know. You might also be trying to figure out what your voice is in this ever-changing realm of social media.

A lot of the micro influencers in our community have a drive to serve and share to help others in any way they can. I often get applicants who aren't sure they are an influencer. Or they don't want to be famous. But they care about helping others who have had similar experiences.

To that, I say: You want to do good for the world? You want to build a financial legacy for yourself, your family, and your community? Hell ya! You are my people. I will help you in every way I can.

YOUR NEAR-FUTURE REALITY

So, let's pretend you're done reading this book. Here is what you can expect once you've read it cover to cover, implemented all the strategies, and started to behave as the smart-as-f*ck, business-savvy, and strategic marketer I know you are.

- ☐ You have an engaged community of followers that is growing at an exponential rate.
- ☐ Your social media friends are equally as obsessed about your niche as you are, whether it is about the best in athleisure fashion, surfing strategies, or as obscure a topic as Bigfoot hunting.
- ☐ Your content is, of course, also epic. So naturally, your engagement rates have spiked. You consistently command an engagement rate two times higher than the industry standard (at minimum) on all your posts. And

since you know how to pitch yourself to the big brands looking for you, you now earn $300 to $10,000 per post. (Seriously, there are influencers out there with fewer than ten thousand followers who charge $7,000 for a thirty-second Reel. Real life. They understand the power of an engaged community. More on that later.)

☐ You have a thriving micro influencer business that you run full-time—or maybe still part-time, but with a plan to ditch your current nine-to-five because it's no longer aligned with your vision for your life.

Yay, you! *Seriously.* A future where you make money using your intellect and creativity and, of course, a cell phone, is yours for the taking. You get to share what you enjoy and are knowledgeable in, and you make a positive difference in the lives of the hundreds of thousands of people who follow you.

Okay, back to now. There's one last thing you need to know. Some people are built for the influencer business. Some are not. You wouldn't be here if you weren't ready for the investment this life requires. It takes guts, determination, and passion to do what you're doing. So I commend you for saying yes when it's so much easier to say no in the face of fear and uncertainty.

Use what you learn here and you will not only perfect your foundation but also skyrocket your engagement, grow your following, and become a professional self-marketer. Most importantly, you will build a sustainable, highly monetizable career in the influencer space.

And *please* remember: persistence wins.

We live in a microwave society where everyone wants immediate results. *Zap! Ten thousand followers and $5,000 for breathing online!* Nope, not so fast. That's not how it works. Overnight coin does not exist.

If you like, you can borrow a mentality I've embraced that's helped me as a marketer. You might need it, too. I remind myself that my one job is to do my best. The goal is to be 1 percent better every day. That is the sole focus.

Now, that doesn't always happen. But I have learned that we always win if we continue to bring our best selves to what we do. I also believe that the universe sends us the experiences we need and the people we need when we need them to shape us. Living this way, I have been blessed to have the opportunity to be a social media marketer for many mega influencers, help thousands of micro influencers, and build a life that truly makes me happy and grows me more each day as a person. This is my calling. And it came over time by being 1 percent better every day and following what I intuitively felt was the right path for me.

You have a calling, too. It's as unique as your DNA. And being an influencer might very well be that. So no more sitting on the sidelines, my friend. No more wondering whether you can do it. You can. All you have to do is decide and commit and put in the work required to do so. This book will take care of the rest.

I will teach you everything you need to know about growing a well-paid influencer and creator career. You will learn the firsthand strategies I implement on some of Instagram's biggest creators' accounts that earn them hundreds of thousands, sometimes millions, of dollars per year.

I will help you evolve. I will help you grow, and also help you refine and rebuild the solid foundation needed this year in order to have a successful account that brands will want to invest in time and time again.

CHAPTER 1

THE LUCRATIVE BUSINESS OF BEING YOU

"The ceiling is short, the field may be long, but the game is wide open!"

—DUDE PERFECT

Do you understand how much power you have at this very moment?

Micro influencers hold all the power with brands today. According to an influencer marketing report conducted by Collabstr, the influencer market went from $9.7 billion in 2020 to $13.8 billion in 2021 and is projected to reach $15 billion by the end of 2022. It grew by 42 percent in only one year. Why? Because it's just smart business. Eighty percent of consumers have purchased a product or service recommended to them by an influencer they follow. My guess is, you don't have to look far to find someone who falls in that category.

Sponcon emerged as a viable business model in the last decade. Ordinary people with engaged online communities are being paid by large corporations—think Nike, Best Buy, and Banana Republic—to promote their products and services. So, it's no surprise that brands have nearly doubled the amount they spend on the creators they activate for their advertising campaigns in the last two years. As this book goes to print, 55 percent of companies have a dedicated budget for content marketing, and nearly four of five allocate funds strictly to influencer marketing.

That trend is growing too. Sixty-six percent of brands are set to increase influencer marketing spend in the next twelve months. Eighty-seven percent use Instagram as their primary advertising avenue. And, according to research conducted by Shopify: "By 2023, brands will spend $4.62 billion per year on influencer marketing...a 25 percent increase between 2021 and 2023."

I am blasting you with stats on purpose. You have to get how massive the business opportunity is right now for you. There has never been a better time to earn a living sharing and teaching others about a topic you love. No question. So please don't go thinking, *I can't make six figures by showing people how to knit headbands*. The odder the niche, the better that might be. I know uncles who are raking in partnership dough because they post pictures of their cute nieces and nephews. From the most odd, to the most random, to the most standard of well-known niches, it all works. Any niche can earn you a living if there is an audience that appreciates it. It is a strange, exciting time for creative entrepreneurial people.

According to the US Bureau of Labor Statistics, the number of Americans who choose self-employment over a corporate position also continues to rise by 7.46 percent each year. Many of these very intelligent people will build personal brands where they get paid to publish. Around 52 percent of them see influencer marketing as a viable career option. Their professional aspiration will be to become full-time content creators.

Since I work with influencers of all kinds, I would bet that the numbers represented by the stats are lower than they are in reality. They should be drastically higher. The reason they aren't is because 68 percent of micro influencers don't believe their work is sufficiently recognized and valued. They aren't running their platforms as a full-time business (though they could). They aren't pitching the right brands, landing deals, or being paid what they are worth. It's also why, despite there being millions of micro influencers, the most significant challenge reported by brands is finding them.

Now imagine you slot your stunning portfolio in the mix. It showcases your niche, the platforms you're passionate about monetizing, the engaged community you have, your creative ability, and the metrics to back it up. You show it to the brand representatives who are sorting through the piles trying to find unicorn micro influencers—savvy social media professionals who offer them strategic exposure and sales. With the strategies you learn in this book, it will be easy for the decision makers to partner with you.

Simply not knowing industry facts keeps most micro influencers from running their dream businesses. It is time for you to be paid what you're worth, and that, my friend, is always more than you think. There are plenty of brands out there who will honor, respect, *and value* your hard work.

Ultimately, building a successful, sustainable influencer career is a five-step formula. Here is what you need to do (and will learn in this book):

1. Follow the damn rules!
2. Understand the reward system.
3. Get clear on YBA (yourself, your brand, and your audience).
4. Continuously create valuable content.
5. Pitch, negotiate, deliver.

First, there are some basics you need to know about the industry and how Instagram works. So we'll start there.

I realize that some people reading this might know aspects of what I am about to tell you already in these first few chapters. If you do, great. Let what you learn be a reminder. But I also have to encourage everyone who is reading this not to skip any of the chapters—even if you think you're ahead of the game and ready to pitch brands. If you're like most of the influencers I work with, you have likely missed critical nuances of the foundational work you have to do to build a sustainable influencer career.

Stay with me. Approach every aspect of this book with an open mind even if you think, *Been there, done that.* You can always further optimize your foundation. Plus, social media is always changing, so if you've been there, done that a few months ago, things have likely changed. Read everything even if you think it's too basic.

We'll start with you having a complete understanding of the landscape of the influencer industry. You will quickly discover how much power you already have—and why it's more than what the mega and macro influencers with sixty thousand or more followers possess.

THE SPECTRUM OF INFLUENCE: MEGA, MACRO, MICRO, NANO

In the world of influencers, there are four types:

1. Mega influencers
2. Macro influencers
3. Micro influencers
4. Nano influencers

Let me break it down for you.

MEGA INFLUENCERS

Mega influencers have one million followers or more. They are the celebrities—the Kylie Jenners, Gary Vees, and Shawn Mendeses of the world. People follow them because they see them in movies or TV, hear them on podcasts, or read about them in magazines. Naturally, due to their widespread fame, they attract a mixed audience with a massive variation in demographics and topics of interest. But it might surprise you to know that mega influencers have massive reach but the least amount of trust.

These people very rarely have a niche, so their relationships with their followers are more distant than the other types of influencers. They are broad personalities with many followers who don't often have relationships with their fellow community members. To their followers, they are characters or the "untouchables." People follow them because their lives are aspirational, not because they seem like actual relatable humans or their friends. There is no sense of community in their social media sphere. Oftentimes, mega influencers approach social media with a "look at me" mentality versus a perspective of "here we are together."

If you ever get sucked into a daydream by the ego aspect of yourself and think, *I wish I had the same level of influence as MrBeast*, that might not be to your advantage. When it comes to brand partnerships, reach isn't as important as an active community. So, that must mean the macro influencers have more power, right? Well, kind of.

MACRO INFLUENCERS

Macro influencers are famous within a niche and have anywhere from one hundred thousand to one million followers. Think of them as mini celebrities. Reality TV stars fit the criteria. For instance, take a former bachelor contestant, Rachael Kirkconnell @rachaelkirkconnell, of ABC's show *The Bachelor* who won the guy prize at the end. She is certainly not as well known as Jake Paul but her content is very high quality. As I was writing this book, she posted a sponsored video about her love of Highline Wellness CBD products so she's definitely earning a decent living as a macro influencer.

Think of macro influencers as semi-untouchable. They don't engage as much with their audience as the influencers with fewer followers because they feel they don't have to. But they do make an effort. Similar to mega influencers, macro influencers have an invisible line between them and their community that communicates, *You follow me, so you're a follower, and I'm an influencer.* Most macro influencers land enough brand deals to earn a handsome living that's easily over six figures annually.

Macro influencers can further be broken down into midtier macro influencers with 20,000-100,000 followers. The midtier macros fit the same profile. Certainly with macros, there's a lesser sense of community than what you would find with a micro influencer.

MICRO INFLUENCERS

Micro influencers have 5,000-20,000 followers; for TikTok, micro influencers have to have 50,000-150,000 followers. This is the category you likely fall into or aspire to. Micro influencers have defined niches. There are micro influencers in all high-earning industries and influencer verticals, such as health and fitness, food, entrepreneurship, fashion, and beauty.

Unlike mega and macro influencers, micro influencers have active and engaged audiences. Said simply, they get the most engagement-worthy comments and shares. Their followers talk to them in the comments section of their posts. More often than not, they respond. A micro influencer might tag followers in their posts. Their members feel like they are their friends. Some of their followers might even know them "personally" on the platform.

The level of engagement micro influencers have with their followers is what is so valuable to brands. Micro influencers have trusted relationships with thousands of people who don't know them in real life but feel connected to them inside the online community they've built. Soon we'll explore how critical engagement is, but for now, consider how hard it might be for a brand to get this same level of trust. It's damn hard! If Instagram could guarantee any brand the same engagement and truth micro influencers have and the fee was $500,000, I don't know any brand that in a heartbeat wouldn't pay it if they had the cash.

An average rule in marketing is that it takes eight to ten touches for most consumers to establish affinity with any brand. Sometimes, it's far more than that. Yet, when a brand sells products through a micro influencer, it can happen in one click. So it's far more effective for a company to pay someone who has that trust already to speak on behalf of their brand than to create those touches from scratch. And micro influencers don't just promote any product. They test, scrutinize, and carefully curate the products and services they share.

There is also a significant difference between influencer giants and micro influencers regarding how they relate to the platform. Macro influencers put coin over community. For micro influencers, it's the other way around; it's community over coin.

Let's pause for a second so you take that in: *community over coin.*

I encourage you to commit that to memory. It will always be a useful focus as you continue to grow.

Micro influencers care more about the people they are impacting than building fame online. Again, this is so desirable for companies. More on that later. But first, what about the nano influencers?

NANO INFLUENCERS

Nano influencers have 1,000–5,000 followers, so you might also currently fall into this category. Nano influencers are day-to-day consumers who are passionate and willing to share. Quite often, nano influencers are broadly referred to as micro influencers. But if you have fewer than 5,000 followers, your ability to make deals with big brands is severely diminished. Though, it's not impossible. In our community, we have quite a few students who have fewer than 5,000 followers and still regularly get paid brand deals. But they could earn far more if they grow.

Nano influencers often don't have a niche yet. They likely haven't figured out a real growth and partnership strategy. They mainly engage with their closest friends and family. They're not necessarily trying to grow, but they still might have decent to high engagement.

While you might aspire to be a mega influencer one day, what you truly want is mega influence. There is a massive difference between the two, and you must get the distinction now, or it will be difficult to succeed as an influencer who can build a sustainable, profitable business long-term.

MEGA INFLUENCER OR MEGA *INFLUENCE*?

In the early days of influencer marketing, follower count was seen by brands as the most important metric. That is no longer the case because engagement rate tends to be higher for micro influencers with smaller communities.

Most mega influencers have horrible engagement rates (like, *are you f*ing kidding* kind of horrible). Yet, brands are paying them *millions*. This is where I choose to not have an out loud opinion on some of the mega influencer deals I have come across. But it blows my mind what brands will pay to be seen. If they are offering millions to mega influencers with terrible engagement, imagine what they would pay to actually achieve real brand engagement.

Engagement rate is also what brands use to analyze how effective a marketing campaign might be. The most common formula for calculating engagement is to add the number of likes and comments on a single post or story then divide that by total number of followers. Then, you multiply that number by one hundred. Here is what that looks like:

$$Engagment\ rate = \frac{Total\ users}{Likes\ per\ post} \times 100$$

As a standard, it's best to calculate engagement monthly or every sixty days. To do that, you need to add up the total likes and comments on every post and divide that number by the total of posts. That will get you the average engagement rate per post. Then you complete the process with the same steps for one post; you divide by total number of followers and multiply by one hundred.

For example, if a micro influencer with 5,000 followers has a total of ten likes and comments on thirty posts, the calculations would look like this:

- 10 likes and comments × 30 posts = 300 likes and comments total for the month
- 300 likes and comments total for the month ÷ 5,000 = 0.06
- 0.06 × 100 = 6 percent

For mega influencers, engagement rate is in the realm of 1–2 percent, which is not good. Many big-name influencers do not have mega*influence.* These people do not have a strong connection with their audience. Because they're celebrities, their fans follow them for entertainment, not because they are real humans they can talk to or learn from.

Mega influencers have giant, semiengaged audiences, while their micro influencer counterparts have two to three times more engagement. Actual influence will make you a sustainable megaearner. And, it's why brands want to work with the micros. It's simply good business sense.

Imagine a team of marketing representatives from the popular clothing brand Madewell evaluating two potential deals, one with a former bachelorette from ABC's hit show *The Bachelorette* and macro influencer Becca Kufrin, or fashion influencer Talya Santos @taylasnts, who posts neutral and relatable fashion. Let's say the social media team responsible for selecting influencers is meeting to review each candidate.

Option A, Kufrin, has 1.3 million followers. She has a 1 percent engagement rate, which would be 13,000 people. Let's say Madewell has to pay her $60,000 for one post and three stories to pose with a new pair of sunglasses that makes $20 profit per pair. For the sake of this exercise, let's pretend the entire 1 percent of engaged community members buy the sunglasses. The most Madewell could make is $26,000.

Option B is Tayla, the micro influencer. She has 33,000 followers, and her engagement rate is 10 percent. She costs $3,000 for one post and three stories. Working with Tayla, Madewell sells 330 pairs of sunglasses at $20 and makes $6,600.

It is pretty apparent what Madewell would do if its business objective was to sell sunnies. If the company worked with Kufrin, it might gain some exposure, but ultimately, it would lose a lot of money. It might make sense for the brand to take a loss over the long-term exposure, but there is no return on investment (ROI) here.

Marketers know consumers need to see a macro or mega influencer with a specific brand for at least a few partnerships before people actually start to trust that the influencer actually believes in the brand and product. So in this instance, they pay Kufrin one time and money is lost. If they pay for a quarter-long contract and she posts two times per month, they still lose a shit ton of money. While, if they pay you—a micro influencer—for a quarter-long deal, they not only make money, they earn engaged brand loyalists. Smart money is good money, and this is the realization many brands are making now.

Most companies are in business to sell products and make money. So, it's easy for them to go with Option B. They could hire thirty-three Taylas for the price of what they would pay Kufrin, engage with 10,890 people, and earn $217,800. Madewell's investment on thirty-three Taylas would be $99,000, but it could profit $118,800.

This scenario shows how follower count is not as important as engagement, and why micro influencers have a significant advantage in the market. For a mega influencer with approximately two hundred million followers, it is not expected that their engagement rate would be any more than 5 percent, whereas that rate is easily doubled for smaller influencers.

Ten micro influencers with communities and followers with more allegiance could be activated for every one mega influencer a brand pays to promote their product. Seasoned micro influencers with high engagement rates can demand anywhere from $300 to $10,000 per post. On average, micro influencers can make $40,000–$100,000 per year with the proper strategy.

People trust micro influencers because of the same psychology as consumer reviews. Most people who shop on Amazon read reviews before they buy. Statistically, females do this before buying products for their kids and animals or anything beauty-related. They want to know what they are putting on their babies. Because people trust people, not brands, if Becky K from Florida says the $200 face cream on Amazon is made of crap and gave her a rash, it's out of your cart. *Nope. I don't need it! It didn't work for Becky K.*

Recommendations will always overshadow the fanciest, most fantastic marketing campaign a brand can run. It's the same in business. A client who speaks highly of me to their friend looking for an influencer marketing agency could easily influence their friend to reach out. They'll want to work with me because their buddy said I was good, not because I'm being all Kanye and advertising that I'm the greatest.

Perception is key. In today's day and age, micro influencers reign supreme because they have brand trust like no other. They are perceived as people "like me," and it's human nature to trust people in similar situations interested in the same stuff we like. So, companies hire micro influencers to share their products and services more than mega influencers because the people following them are interested in similar brands, products, and experiences.

And the only reason a micro influencer, like you, works with a brand is that you like the product and believe in what they're doing. It's not solely for the money, because you are involved with your community. Have you ever seen the Aveeno commercials Jennifer Aniston does and think, *Is her bathroom really full of Aveeno?* Could be, but I highly doubt it. Let's be honest, most of us aren't buying it. You would rarely think that when you see a micro influencer promote a product. You trust they use it and love it. You can almost see the spark of truth in their eyes when they share a video about it. And that's how micro influencers create megainfluence.

YOU GOTTA E.A.T.

Micro influencers are a discerning bunch, and brands and followers alike appreciate that. As a micro influencer, you carefully scrutinize and curate (or should, and we'll get there) the best products and only share what is useful and meaningful to you and in your opinion would benefit your audience. Ninety-nine percent of micro influencers say they believe in the products and services they promote, unlike mega influencers, which is why brands love and need you! But there are so many of you that it's hard for brands to comb through the crowd to find their ideal candidates. That is why you must go to them.

Because of the brand trust you have, when a brand works with you, they bypass a shit ton of work and reduce their spend to gain exposure. With you, there's little hesitation, so they can skip multiple steps. You are much more relatable to consumers than any mega or macro influencer celebrities. And, if you do it right, you will maintain that relatability as you grow, which brings me to my next point on this: you gotta remember to E.A.T.

Micro influencers E.A.T. more than anyone else on the platform. The E.A.T. acronym is marketing nerd speak to describe the essential characteristics brands look for in business partners. The acronym was created by Google and is the basis for its search algorithm. E.A.T. stands for: expertise, authority, trustworthiness.

In the context of Google, if you use the search bot to find a product like "best teeth whitener" because you want whiter pearls, the technology behind the Google search engine will pull up the best sites that fit the E.A.T. criteria. In other words, the sites with enough expert content that show authority and trust because lots of people visit them and spend time on these sites, are ranked top in your browser. They are sites that meet the E.A.T. criteria. These same characteristics—expertise, authority, trustworthiness—are the key characteristics a brand looks for when they choose micro influencers as partners. Ultimately, your focus must be to become an *expert* that has *authority* and *trust* with your audience.

A successful micro influencer has a niche where they have demonstrated *expertise*, either by what they know or because they constantly post content related to it. People follow them because they enjoy this particular topic, so they have *authority* through a community that listens to them. They show *trust* because people continuously engage with the content that they are producing. Do this, and you are every brand's ideal representative without costing hundreds of thousands of dollars.

A strategic use of micro influencers creates a powerful level of brand awareness. Companies can expand by tapping into a more specific demographic within their general prospecting pool than what they would get with world-famous influencers or in advertising alone. Nearly two out of every three consumers say they trust influencer messages about a brand more than a company's advertising about their products. And soon, you will learn how to streamline your reach-out process and ensure you drastically increase your engaged following and engagement and brand partnership close rate.

As a micro influencer, the business opportunity you have here is insane. You can't put a price on brand trust. As a marketer, I can tell you that the cost per thousand impressions (CPM)—which is a measurement used in marketing to calculate how many thousands of people your advertising or marketing piece has left an impression on—is ridiculous today because the competition is so high. There are probably millions of e-commerce brands out there trying to get new people to care about their brand. If you have enough trust where someone who follows you will listen, click, and buy, why would a company not pay you for that?

Now, above all else, you have to follow the rules and understand Instagram's reward system so you know how to win.

INFLUENCER SUCCESS BASICS: AVOID PISSING OFF THE POWERS THAT BE (A.K.A. INSTAGRAM)

You know this, I'm sure, but we all have moments where we get frustrated with some process and consider hacking a system to get ahead faster. We all do it at one point or another and it will always cost you more in the long run than it will help you in the short run.

People want what they want faster than what reality provides. Again, I know you know, but I need to say this up front so we can move on from the foundational ground rules to the accelerated strategies that will earn you money.

I would fail you if I didn't say this, even though I know you know not to do it: never buy followers. Do not violate Instagram's terms of use. All social media apps have terms of service. Read them. Seriously, please read them. Not kidding.

You could build an active community, but you have a misstep or two and Instagram shuts your ass down. And then, there's no crying to get back on. The company doesn't need your money. Or your followers. You don't want bad blood with the social media gods, so play by the rules.

When you download any application, you sign a contract saying, *I will follow your rules.* You and I are never in charge. Instagram rules its platform. So play by its rules, and you will be rewarded and make money while you do it. This is essential to the longevity of your Instagram influencer career. If you have not read the Instagram terms of use, either Google it or check the help section of Instagram. Get familiar with its terms of use and check back often because it is constantly being updated.

Understand that Instagram's priorities as an organization are to:

1. Make sure its features work effectively and efficiently.
2. Filter out accounts that cause users to leave the platform.

Spamming users messes with the Instagram user experience. Instagram will—100 percent—punish you for such behavior, so don't do it. Meta, the owner of Instagram and Facebook, does not play around. What follows are common pitfalls I've seen micro influencers fall into. Best to know them now so you can sidestep significant issues in the future.

PITFALL #1: USING EXTERNAL GROWTH AUTOMATIONS

Instagram hates bots and has stringent automation guidelines due to recent updates. It recently changed its algorithm to highly favor genuine engagements in order to combat illegal use of the platform. Any opportunity (and there are many) to "crack the code" of Instagram growth is a short-term fix. According to Instagram's user agreement, these methods are considered black hat and are not a sustainable means for growth. The company will shadowban you (we'll cover that soon) and stop offering your content at any moment, which you cannot afford.

Do not participate in massive story watching, automated power likes, automated followers, or mass bot commenting. Never DM the same message to multiple people over and over again. Never DM the same message to multiple people over and over again. See how uncool that is? That is how you get blocked.

Instagram views these actions as inauthentic and highly spammy. It doesn't like you using a bot for spamming five million strangers with a notification of you viewing their stories. And it makes sense because that's not why the platform was created. So never invest in companies that use growth hacks. It's a bad idea for the longevity of your influencer career. Instead, build genuine connections with users. Remember, Instagram's algorithm is robust, precise, and always iterating. Don't fight the system. Flow with it.

If you want Instagram to favor your content and maximize your growth, your focus is to maintain your IG trust score. Your IG trust score is how Instagram ranks your profile. Think of it like a credit score. Positive actions strengthen your score. Negative actions lower it. You are either ranked as a trustworthy or a spam-like account at risk of getting banned. Instagram analyzes every action you take on the platform. Depending on the quality of these actions, your IG trust score can rise or drop at any moment.

There's no specific or technical way of checking your exact IG trust score, but if your account gets blocked often or Instagram forbids you to perform specific actions, you're likely to be interpreted by Instagram as spam, which you do not want.

PITFALL #2: NOT DELETING YOUR GHOST FOLLOWERS

Everyone has ghost followers. They are people that follow you but don't engage. Set aside time once a month to remove inactive or ghost followers from your list. You must do this if you are serious about landing lucrative brand deals. Get rid of them, because they skew your engagement rate. A bad engagement rate due to ghosts reduces your opportunity to pop up in the search feature of the platform. Ghosts will scare potential brand partners away.

Instagram also does a decent job of regularly removing some of these users from your account, which is excellent. It's why you might wake up one morning and see you've lost fifty to one hundred followers randomly overnight—Instagram deletes fake accounts. Some external apps can do this for you too, but I can't say with certainty they work or remove only ghost followers, so it's best not to use them. Dedicate time monthly to deleting ghosts manually. If there is a suspect account with no profile picture and hardly any followers but who follows five thousand accounts, that is a ghost to delete. So, grab a snack, turn on some Netflix, and go on a blocking spree.

Now, let's address what to do if you feel you've been shadowbanned from Instagram—because that will affect your performance on the platform and your ability to land deals.

PITFALL #3: ACCIDENTAL SHADOWBAN

Shadowban is not an official Instagram term. Users use it to describe when Instagram deprioritizes accounts on the app. It doesn't cancel your account, but it significantly limits your reach and exposure so you get far fewer likes. Being shadowbanned can decrease reach, limit who can see your posts, and seriously affect engagement without warning or notice. It can make your content (or account) undiscoverable via hashtags and the explore page.

In extreme cases, content is taken down completely. You can also be locked out of your account. If that happens, it's because you violated one or more of Instagram's terms of use. Here are five of the most common ways to be shadowbanned so you avoid it:

#1. Posting inappropriate content. Posts with violence, sexually suggestive content, or misinformation are no-nos.

#2. Paying for likes or comments or use bots to increase followers or participate in engagement pods. Don't use software that violates Instagram's terms of use, such as bot software. Only use official Instagram partner apps like Later and ManyChat. To find out if you have any bot services or unapproved apps linked to your account, go to your Instagram settings, tap Security, and then Apps and Websites. Here, you'll be able to see all of the active apps your account uses, any that have expired, and those you've removed.

#3. Acting spammy. Avoid spam-like activity, such as copying and pasting the same comment or DM or following and unfollowing accounts. Using over thirty hashtags in a single post, for instance, is not a good move. Some creators have been shadowbanned for commenting on too many posts or following too many people within an hour. It may be interpreted as bot activity if you suddenly follow fifty accounts or like too many posts.

#4. Using banned hashtags. There is no official Instagram list of hashtags to avoid, but marketers know there are hashtags Instagram has banned. They range from the obvious don't use words to ones you might question. Here are don't use hashtags: #alone #curvygirls, #nasty, #brain, #master, #lulu. Ideaco.co often posts the hashtags to avoid and they update their site frequently so visit them for more on hashtags. Check your hashtag groupings regularly to determine if the hashtag has any recent posts you are using. Or get an account with Flick Tech and plug your hashtag groupings there to find out if you are using banned hashtags.

It is so important to audit the hashtags you use regularly. Search for them on Instagram. If the Top Posts section appears but nothing else, it's likely been banned. Sometimes Instagram will leave a short message on the Hashtag page explaining that posts have been hidden for not meeting community guidelines.

If a hashtag you frequently use is suddenly banned, remove it from your recent posts and keep an eye on whether the ban is lifted in the future. If that doesn't work, remove all the hashtags from your most recent posts ASAP. Go back and delete at least a month's worth of hashtags. This works well for most people pretty quickly. Then when you go to post again, change up the number of hashtags you use and put your hashtags in your post instead of the comment section if you've been doing that.

#5. Using a hashtag that receives a sudden surge of activity. Instagram will likely detect the flurry of activity as spam and hide all posts associated with that hashtag.

If you think you've been shadowbanned, don't delete your account. First, make sure the app is up to date. If you are using an older version, you might simply have a technical problem. If that is *not* the case, reach out to Instagram. Plead your case. Also, do not beat yourself up. It happens more frequently than you know. It sucks, but it can typically be reversed relatively quickly.

To report your shadowban to Instagram, go to your Instagram Settings, tap Help, and select Report a Problem. A pop-up will appear with a few options. Choose "Something Isn't Working" and write a message describing your issue.

Sometimes an Instagram vacation is the solution. Many influencers have taken a few days off of Instagram, and it lifted their shadowban. I suggest a week break if you really think you've been shadowbanned. The key is not to post, comment, or even log onto the app during that time. After your break, there's a chance you can go back to liking and posting as you usually would.

One question I always get is: how long does an Instagram shadowban last? Truly, no one knows. It's rumored to get lifted within two to three weeks. However, I've heard horror stories of it lasting a month or longer. So, behave well on the platform and stay informed. Engage with people manually. It might take more time and effort, but it proves to Instagram that you're abiding by their terms of use.

Ignorance of the rules and regulations is zero excuse with Instagram, so study up and be a rule-abiding user. Now, let's get you familiar with how Instagram's reward system works as a second fundamental.

UNDERSTAND THE REWARD SYSTEM

To be successful on the platform, you must understand Instagram's reward system. It will honor you for keeping people on the platform because that is how the company makes money. The more people stay to engage with your content, the more opportunities they have to serve them ads, which earn them a shit ton—literally billions of dollars. Trust me. I produce millions of dollars in social media ad revenue a year for my clients. My job is to understand the Instagram algorithm and use that knowledge to build effective Instagram ad campaigns. So, remember: keep people on the platform. It will serve you wonders.

Instagram wants its creators to be authentic and entertaining. You will be rewarded for being creative and driving traffic to your page. Suppose Instagram notices significant traffic is consistently being driven to your profile. In this case, it will promote your content to a greater reach within your audience and explore pages and rank relevant hashtags, causing your account to experience exponential growth. The more Instagram users search your account and spend time looking at your photos, videos, and stories, the more you'll be rewarded with exposure.

Whenever Instagram releases a new feature, use it. This is crucial. The algorithm rewards you the more you interact with it. So, be an A-plus student. Using new features proves to Instagram that you love its platform and want everyone to spend time there.

Build a true community and you'll have ever-growing engagement. The best way to do this is to get people to stop and hang on your post or profile for a minute or two. Ultimately, your goal is to increase that average every day. More on epic content in Chapter 4.

In the end, always remember that Instagram is in charge. It owns the platform. People surprisingly get very offended when it takes action against them. Instagram is not a democracy, like the United States of America. It is a dictatorship. What it wants goes. You signed a contract to download their app so any time you are frustrated and act out in ways the platform is against, it will punish or delete your account. Although Instagram doesn't run like America, remember it is still a land of opportunity for those who are strategic.

DO THIS NOW:

- Where do you fall on the spectrum of influence? Nano? Micro? Macro? Take note of where you are and think about the next level you'd like to get to. What's your next target?
- Have you read the Instagram terms of use? If not, do that now. Always review your content and daily habits on the platform to ensure you are in line with Instagram's guidelines.
- Do an audit of your account and remove anyone who seems like a ghost follower. To make this a regular habit, schedule it. Do it every month.

CHAPTER 2

UNCOVER YOUR NICHE

"In order to find yourself, who you really are, you got to be with yourself; you got to hang out with yourself."

—POST MALONE

Why do you want to be an influencer?

When I ask micro influencers this question, one common answer is, *To make a lot of money and be famous.* And that's when I know they will fail. This line of thinking never leads to a sustainable business. Instead, they will more likely drive themselves crazy. While they might make decent money for a short period of time, they will surely never achieve the fulfillment they ultimately seek.

Ninety percent of micro influencers are not as successful as they could be because they have not done a deep enough exploration and analysis of the two foundational components—both related to a person's why—required to build a sustainable influencer business. They are:

1. Niche
2. Audience

Even people who *think* they have done the work have typically made assumptions. They are missing the mark, and it's costing them brand deals and thousands of dollars every year. Most micro influencers have not done enough homework to uncover their ultimate whys and understand their niche. If you do not have a deep understanding of your why and niche, you might still acquire an audience but it will be more on a superficial level and that is hard to monetize.

Most influencers join our community and attend our Micro Influencer Academy because they do not feel self-expressed on the platform or they are frustrated about not being compensated for their creativity and the community they have built. They are not seeing the engagement rates they'd like to see or having the impact they envision. It comes back to these two foundational elements that set the successful micro influencers with sustainable businesses apart from the rest. So the next two chapters come with a disclaimer: do not skip this work.

You might be reading this and thinking, *I've heard this before.* You might think you are a master of social media. You know your brand and audience, right? If so, great, but there is always another layer to learn. When it comes to being an influencer—or being in any line of business for that matter— nothing stays the same. You are constantly changing, and so is your industry and the needs of the people you serve.

It breaks my heart when intelligent, talented, highly capable influencers *think they know* their niche and audience but are so off track. You should constantly monitor metrics, follow the latest trends, and reflect on your niche and audience. If those two components aren't thoroughly formed, your efforts are a waste of time. Passion is incredible, but a poorly developed strategy will not get you where you want to go.

It's a common mistake. We have all been passionate about something and headed down a wrong path at one point— anyone else ever professed your love for a "forever soulmate," but you now cringe thinking about how wrong the relationship was for you? (Currently, I do this about once per year; pray for me!) I have to have an IG big sister moment here and say: I love you, you're very passionate about this one thing, but if you're going to make something of yourself, you need to focus, get clear on implementation, and do the work! Be a business person. End rant.

I see people fail from this all the time. If you have no clarity around what you're offering, or why brands should want to work with you, you will not be successful as an influencer. It's fantastic that your Instagram is all about fashion but anyone can do that. Who is your niche-specific audience, the people your account speaks to? If it's women's street wear then it makes sense why Zara (or another similar brand) might want to work with you. If you have no idea, you've got work to do. What if everyone who follows you is under eighteen, and you want to promote your personal line of $98 hoodies? That is probably not going to do well. And then, imagine you take it further and invest $10,000 in apparel that your audience can't afford. I hope you love hoodies, because you now have an entire closet.

The work of these chapters is not above or below anyone. You could be a multimillionaire. You could be very experienced in business. But you now want to be an influencer. Your niche and audience matter. So again, please do not skip these chapters.

You might need to conjure up a greater level of self-discipline at this moment to overcome the "yeah, I know" mindset that trips us all up. I've been there too. I still have these moments, but I always try to center myself and say, *No, I can indeed learn something new today from this because I am open to see things in a new light, from another qualified perspective.* I've read motivational books where I blazed past stuff I've heard before. Yeah, yeah, I get it. Five minutes of gratitude is important. I heard it before. Then months later, I'm in a funk. I pick the book up and finally get the message and finally implement the practice. And then, my life is so much better because I took five minutes to listen. It's easy to sidestep this work, but just as easy to do it.

Typically, anything approached as a new learner offers deeper levels of value. When I read motivation and business books multiple times I always learn something new. Why? Because I'm constantly changing every day. Learning yesterday is different from learning today because what I experienced yesterday now applies to today. Same for you.

Stay with me. You will learn something new, and it will make a difference. Let's start with why you are doing this.

WHY DO YOU WANT THIS, REALLY?

Everybody wants to be an influencer nowadays, but most people genuinely don't know *why* they want to be one. Having the conversation with yourself as to why you want this—outside of the ability to make your own schedule, work online, and make money from anywhere in the world—is essential.

Money and fame are not the real reason for anyone to become an influencer. These are surface-level desires that are nice and that most of us would like to have but they are really just byproducts of a deeper conviction and purpose. It is okay to want them, but at the end of the day, if it's about followers and being rich, it's not sustainable. You won't put in the work when you don't feel like it or when a task seems too challenging. Watch the latest episode of your favorite show or send pitches out to thirty brands?

It's like working out at the gym. You're not getting a six-pack by chilling and drinking a six-pack. You get shredded because you commit to the process of regularly working hard, lifting weights, and being extremely intentional with the foods you put into your mouth on a daily basis.

At your core, this is not about getting more followers or more money, truly. Those are byproducts of survival needs. All humans have five basic desires: survival, esteem, mating, freedom, meaning.

Not having a sustainable reason will drive you crazy. Chasing money will cause you to always be internally frustrated. It's never enough. When life doesn't go your way, which is life, it will feel like it's destroying you.

I have been there. Early in my career, I lost one of my biggest clients because they sold their company. I had been making $30,000 a month and that number went to zero. Suddenly, I was rich-broke. It devastated me because I didn't understand how I could "fail" so hard. But I had also been living beyond my means. Everything was about money and my company.

As I get older, I want to always remain in a great place financially. The goal is to have the funds to travel, pay my bills, invest, bless my friends and family and community, and give my dog the view he deserves. That is the important stuff to me. I don't need to be rich. I need to be more than well off. Would I enjoy more f*ck-you money, as I call it? (By the way, f*ck-you money means having enough in the bank to do whatever you want or say buh bye to any job you hate.) Sure, but it's not my goal. My goal is to find my why and that always allows me to remain grounded and focused on the true goal. Nowadays, I care about legacy and leaving the world a better place for my family, friends, future kids, and community. The focus is wealth—monetary and other—not for ego or greed but for security and contribution. When people stop focusing on the superficial parts of success and instead understand why they want to serve from a legacy perspective in a way that is aligned with helping people, they become more effective in building a sustainable business. I don't know why the universe works this way, but it does.

On the money front, before I continue, there is nothing wrong with wanting money. Everyone needs it to live. It's okay to want an abundant life. Some people think having too much money is greedy, but there's a difference between having wealth and being rich. Wealth is what I believe is money's intended use. A wealth of anything requires hard work, time, and patience. It requires consistency above all else. The people who I work with that are incredibly successful will tell you the same. They are focused on sustainable wealth.

And usually building wealth is easier when work and life become about people and the journey. When dreams are pursued with an understanding that great things take time, it just works. You succeed. So focus on why that's bigger than you. You are here to serve a group you care about in a way you care about with a gift you possess.

Social media too often feeds the mentality of our subconscious—and hell, sometimes extremely conscious—demand for wanting success *now*. There are influencers who were nobodies three years ago, and now they are running the highlights from New York Fashion Week. To keep your head on straight in this industry and for business (and life) success, you need to have a more profound reason than making money or being Insta famous. Everything is easier when you are grounded in a reason that's centered on service to others and what you believe is your purpose on the planet. If you knew you would have to send out four hundred pitches in three months and only land three, would you do it? Maybe not, unless you know why, and you know it in your gut.

So, sit with yourself for a moment: why do you want to grow your influencer career?

If your first answer to that question isn't a place of sustainability or if it seems too superficial, unpack it. What's the why beneath that why? Continue to ask yourself this question regularly. It's extremely healthy to do so. It will look something like this:

Self: Why do you want to grow your influencer career?

Inner voice: *To make money from my phone!*

Self: Great! Now, why else?

Inner voice: *Because then I could quit working this job I hate.*

Self: Another plus. What's another reason?

Inner voice: *Honestly, it would be amazing if I could get a bigger apartment so my sister could stay with me.*

Self: Anything else?

Inner voice: *I'm really scared about my sister commuting. I need to get a bigger place.*

Self: Anything else?

Inner voice: *I freaking love marketing. It would be really fun to run my own agency.*

Self: Anything else?

Inner voice: *I'd love to be an example for my sister and other women and show them what's possible when you love what you do.*

Self: Now, why?

Inner voice: *Because I believe in dreams and that anyone can live the life they want. If I believe it and want to empower anyone, I need to be that.*

I went through a similar line of thinking when I started my agency. Do this work with yourself and keep going until you run out of answers for why. Eventually, you will get to a reason that is as unique as your DNA. It will come from a deep place inside you that seems like it's connected to your soul—not your followers or bank account.

Maybe you want to take care of yourself and your loved ones. Or you want to feel as though you always bring deep value to any table. Or maybe, you want to be your best self to attract the same in a partner. And if you had all that, what would your why be then? Maybe then you could focus on the impact you want to have on your friends, family, and the world at large. You want a life of freedom that you sometimes think is only within reach in your dreams, but deep down, you know it's not. You know you can obtain it. You just need guidance (and I've got your back there).

A purpose like that helps you keep going. Keep asking why until you no longer have an answer. When you get there, that is your reason. And it matters. Write it down. You will need to come back to it on days where you are not motivated or when it changes (because you will change). Come back to the question again.

Now, since being an influencer is a business, how do you connect that reason to a passion where you profit? For that, you need to identify your niche, or your gifted monetizable passion.

YOUR GIFTED MONETIZABLE PASSION

Brands want to make money, so they only partner with people who understand their niche and share relevant content. So, after you have asked the question, "Why do I want to be an influencer?" next ask, "What am I good at?"

The wise philosopher Socrates once said, "Know thyself," and it's advice that certainly applies to influencers where your business is you. You need to have a serious heart-to-heart with yourself about the topics you genuinely love. Do not replicate the niches of other influencers just because they have made it.

I highly recommend that influencers read *Good to Great*—an incredible book by business management expert Jim Collins, speaking to the difference between good and great companies. At So Social, we use the same words, good and great, to define ourselves and influencers. Great influencers have successfully combined their passion with a topic they are obsessed about so they want to learn and share. They combine that with smart marketing strategy, and bingo—it's the formula for success. As an equation, it would look something like this:

Passion + Desire to learn and share +
Success-proven strategy = Success!

Great influencers focus their brand on topics they can easily be passionate about, what they can be one of the best in the world at, and that drives their ability to make money. They choose a niche that is an expression of them. Passion combined with a desire to learn and share—and then considered in relation to business markets—will get you to your gifted monetizable passion.

It's not enough to have a passion. You need to want to be knowledgeable inside the niche you chose. Knowledge doesn't get you anywhere without sharing it. So, a topic you're passionate about *and* want to be an expert in enough to share everything you learn is an ideal niche. You might have many, but there will be one for you that stands out.

If you're not excited about a particular topic, you're not going to want to create content about it every day. On Instagram, you will need to post stories every day. For TikTok, you should be posting at least *two to five videos* every day. If you hate the subject you're sharing about, it will get old quickly. Don't mirror someone else's success unless you also share that same passion, because you won't be able to fake that much content. (And you can't just share a passion for the influencer lifestyle. You have to resonate with their content if you're going to model yourself after them.)

Be all things to all people, and you speak to no one. You have to be yourself. So what are you good at? What comes naturally to you?

My best advice is, don't stress. Too many influencers get in their heads when I ask them this question. They get overly analytical and logical. If you love watercolors, don't immediately default to, *I can't earn a living teaching people to paint pictures online.* That is not true. There are hundreds of influencers teaching people how to paint with watercolors. We'll get to the money factor shortly.

Great influencers are passionate about what they are focused on, so it's easy to create content even when they have a content block because they love what they are learning regardless of what they are getting paid. In one of the first training sessions of Built to Influence Academy, I ask students the question: What would you talk about regardless of whether you're paid for it or not? This is the greatest differentiating factor between good and great influencers.

The service you provide as an influencer is the training or entertainment value you give to a community. Ultimately, that is what brands pay you for too.

Maybe you are passionate about food. Well, everybody loves food. We need it to survive. It's not a bad niche. However, you need to assess whether you love it enough to visit restaurants and post about them. Or explain the properties of what makes a great pasta over one that's subpar. Do you love pizza enough to own the pizza space? (By the way, pizza is the most hashtagged food on Instagram.)

If you like a topic and have a desire to become an expert in that space, that's the sweet spot. Followers don't want to align with somebody who isn't also knowledgeable. They might follow you because you are entertaining, but they are also following you to get value, and that value is given and received by the transfer of knowledge.

Don't overanalyze what education is on social media. If you want to be an expert on #forks you probably could. No joke, I legit looked that up after writing it because I got curious. I searched #forks and found a very informative Instagram

Reel that taught me that the best way to organize cutlery in a tray is by standing it up on its side versus laying it flat and piling it up! Who knew? And by the way, I hope that guy gets more strategic because a cutlery company would have 100 percent paid him to do a sponsored post version of that video and people would have eaten it up.

Consider fashion. If you are interested in fashion and styling, you really want to teach people how to look great. Or, if gaming is your thing, you should be posting tutorials of you playing. If personal growth is your niche, maybe you're sharing thinking hacks and tools.

It doesn't have to be hard to educate others, and it shouldn't if you love what you are doing. People crave new knowledge innately, and social media is a beautiful platform for knowledge transfer. Being an influencer is powerful. You can teach people what they want to know or didn't even know they needed to know, and you can do it in a fun way. They often won't even realize that they are learning something new.

Great influencers also stay on-brand. They clearly understand their niche and stick to it. Without a clearly defined niche, you'll never make as much money as you possibly could. A good influencer might have a pleasant personality, take good shots, and be entertaining—and they'll make money here and there, even if they do not have a clearly defined niche.

Ask yourself these questions:

- What are you good at?
- What do you enjoy doing?

- What are you easily well-versed in?
- How can this skill help other people?

Once you define what you are good at and enjoy doing that helps other people, *voila*! That is your gifted monetizable passion and niche. It's the space where you are most authentic—where your passion bleeds into a desire to share that thing with other people in a way that they will pay attention (and even pay you) for that knowledge.

Good influencers are seasonal. They are the people who get canceled all the time. You can be popular today and nonexistent tomorrow. The people I have seen this happen to did not have a clear niche. They were famous for one piece of content or one video, and then someone hotter or brighter or more entertaining came along and wiped them out. Don't let that be you.

So, are there brands relative to that niche? If there aren't, then that's probably not a viable monetizable passion for an influencer.

People often tell me they don't have a niche. Most of the time that is not true. They simply haven't thought deeply about it. And only then can you think about niching down.

YOUR NICHE WITHIN A NICHE

If you define your niche in the most granular terms, you can find a monetizable, high-engagement sweet spot. To get there, you want to know that people are looking for what you want to offer them, which requires a bit of intelligent digging.

Let's go back to the #fork example. You have a passion for forks and want to be an influencer in the cutlery space. Well, are there enough people searching for information about the right forks to buy? Are fork companies looking for influencers to promote their products? Probably! And if they aren't they likely just don't know they have potential brand representatives on social media. Now, will being a #fork influencer make you millions? Probably not. (I dare anyone to prove me wrong.) The most random topics are monetizable these days. But be smart and do your research. A simple Instagram search in your niche will help you zero in on your territory within your niche.

I enjoy social media marketing, but my other biggest passion is relaxation. And even though I love relaxing probably more than work, it's not in my monetized bubble or a gifted passion of mine. See how that doesn't count? Now, you might be thinking that I could partner with sleep doctors that preach relaxation and build funny videos about chilling out. So relaxation may very well be a monetizable niche. In fact, everything can be in a monetized bubble if you get creative enough. Before you start posting content, just do your research to figure out what that bubble is. Gather evidence, so you don't waste time and money. The point is if you go too niche it'll be a problem. No one will want what you offer.

Recently, a student who attended our Micro Influencer Academy went too narrow with her niche and was struggling. She was a mom of foster children who offered school hacks for kids in grade twelve. Only kids in grade twelve? I told her not to get so granular that she missed out on so many other people that she could help. She had raised her kid since age five and had experience with school-aged kids from kindergarten to grade twelve. So she pivoted. She started offering tips that helped foster moms do day-to-day life with their kids, and now she speaks to all foster moms providing value where they need it instead of one particular area that caters to too little a crowd.

The key is to find a sweet spot where the niche isn't too small but also not too wide open that you enter an overly saturated market. For instance, fitness influencers are in a super-oversaturated niche. So if you want to step into it, you would think about the angle of the fitness space you are knowledgeable in, passionate about, and could own. Maybe you want to be successful in mommy fitness for women who have just had babies. It's still a vast audience, but specific enough that you can stand out. A million moms fall into that category of women who just had a baby and want to get back in shape. Maybe it's their first kid and they want a fitness expert who understands them, and you've had three.

Or what about being a fitness trainer who specializes in women and men transitioning gender? I know an influencer who niched down and is very successful. There are so many people transitioning who feel uncomfortable at gyms. She understood because she had life experience.

Fitness is a gazillion-dollar industry, but if you start looking through the fitness hashtag, which probably 200 million people use, you see smaller segments within the large audience.

Now, there is nothing wrong with having multiple interests. It's completely natural and very human. You will have to decide which one you're going to focus on first. What are you *most* passionate about? Likely most people are passionate about one over the other. So pick that, get some proof that it's a monetizable concept, build that out.

Suppose you're a foodie but also like dogs and are considering either one as a niche. Congrats, you have great taste and therefore represent like 98 percent of the population. Pick one: pooch pics or pasta? You are welcome to create a career with different verticals and accounts you're trying to scale, but win at one first to avoid confusing people. Focus on one niche, scale it until it's working, and then duplicate your process of engagement and brand reach-outs. Then keep building in verticals that you like.

BE A VALUE-BASED INFLUENCER

Attention and true influence are very different metrics. Brands care about actionable data. Do you have your audiences' attention, or do you influence their decisions? The reason your focus is to provide value and not just entertainment is because value-based influencers are listened to and taken seriously by their followers.

Most people are over the hot girl or boy influencer who only offers cute pictures. I see way too many influencers with profiles that communicate, *I'm hot, so you should follow me.* Congrats, how else can you capture my attention? You may be nice to look at, but that type of influencer career is not sustainable. A new hot person pops up every other day on the platform. If the premise of your account is superficial, expect only superficial influence.

If that's where you're at in your influencer journey, I'm not trying to make you feel bad, but I do want you to wake up to find a proper niche and real expertise based on a passion you can share. The influencer game is worse than professional sports when it comes to who "makes it." The court of public opinion on Instagram will trade you in a minute if you don't adapt. Brands pay influencers well when they capture, hold, and grow *influence*, not attention. They have the Jenners to pay for that.

I only rag on building a brand around hotness simply because it is not effective long-term. Now, there is nothing wrong with it if you plan on being a well-paid professional model, or if you don't care to make money and just want to be famous for being hot. Nothing wrong with that if it's your goal. But ultimately, value-based influencers win. Many people like and engage with the content of influencers who look good. However, very few will buy from them. Their target audience is simply interested in their six-pack abs and bikinis. I know many hot boy girl mega influencers who cannot sell for shit. Why? They don't hold real influence within their communities.

Alongside hotness, you should also move past your sex, gender, race, sexual orientation, and relationship status. It is beautiful to be a part of any group, but belonging to those groups doesn't make you an authority figure; it makes you human. Looks are not enough to be a trustworthy authority figure. Experience and connection are necessary.

You bought this book, so you have deep goals and dreams. Let's figure out together how to reach them. The first is to sit with yourself and define your goal on your Instagram account. Where do you want to take it in the next two years? What value can and do you bring? Be brutally honest with yourself. Is your account basic, and you're only attracting looky-loos? If you are, that's okay. We can fix that.

If you're doing it right, your brand partnership campaigns produce high-value user-generated content (UGC) that inspires your audience to follow, buy from, post and tag a brand. Meanwhile, you are giving your audience insider access to your life and the brands you love and work with, and that kind of front-row seat into your life is priceless to them.

Unless you're a megacelebrity, attention is not your play. Influence is. Attention is freely given in today's market. Influence is earned through you niching down and investing the time and resources to provide true value to your audience.

Most influencers stop at being likable and trustworthy. But that isn't hard. You can like me and trust me as a human, but not give me the authority in your life to suggest a product, brand or service, or experience. You only get that when you reveal yourself. You have to graduate to the next step, build credibility, which only happens through shared experience, your ability to prove results, and your ability to speak to a topic. Define your gifted monetizable passion and the value you offer to a specific audience. And then, it'll be much easier to figure out your brand identity.

YOUR BRAND IMAGE

Your gifted monetizable passion should further define your

brand to leave a strong impression on your audience and the companies you want to work with. Authenticity, creativity, and passion show through on social media, so it's important to build a brand that reveals that within you. Let your brand show your audience who you are.

The question is always, *How the heck do you figure that out?* But it's easier than you think. Start by looking at the profiles of influencers in your niche. In Chapter 3, we'll talk more about this when we identify Your Hero 100—they are the competitors you'd like to be like who are in your niche. To start, visit the profiles of your competition. Look at their color schemes, videos, and style of photos. Do you like them? Keep track of what appeals to you and also what you hate. Then, audit their posts.

How much engagement are particular posts getting? If they're getting a lot of engagement, there's no harm in swiping that color palette or going to similar hues or content topics. You don't have to reinvent the wheel. It's about what your audience likes, and winning influencers in your space have likely done a great deal of work already to identify what followers vibe with.

If you are thinking, *I haven't defined my niche enough yet and don't have an audience*, we will dive deep into that in the next chapter. What I'll say now is that if you have a random audience, that's fine. Starting from zero is a great place to be. If you look at a person's profile and think, *I freaking want that person's life...and the community they have...and the partnerships they have...and aesthetic*, again, don't reinvent the wheel. It's working for them. They've done the hard part for you. Draw inspiration from them. Never guess. You might love neon orange, but does your audience? If not, paint an accent wall in your house orange and use another color on Instagram.

Your image must also be cohesive. Streamline all your profiles: Facebook, YouTube, LinkedIn, everything. What's cool about TikTok is that it often emulates Instagram. Google yourself and make sure you appear cohesive everywhere. The profile photo you use on every platform should be the same and so should the colors and vibe. Think brand continuity. Also, keep everything up to date.

Your image should be cohesive but not overproduced. You want to be clean and consistent but also raw, accurate, and genuine—so limit overediting. Neither platform favors a highly produced look.

Take some time to really sit with this one—thoroughly process and define your brand voice, and if you've done it previously, reevaluate what you created before to make sure you are still optimized for best performance. The questions that follow will help greatly when it comes to appropriately identifying your audience, which we'll do next in Chapter 3.

DO THIS NOW

- What's your why? Ask yourself this question and keep going until you run out of answers. When you feel deeply moved by the reason you get to, that is it! Write it down so it stays top of mind.
- Identify your gifted monetizable passion. What niche are you passionate about, that you also want to be an expert in, and that there is a demand for?

- What's your brand vibe? Use the questions below to consider all angles of your brand. If you are having a hard time figuring out your brand vibe, read Chapter 3 and come back to these questions. Learning about your audience (the work of the next chapter) might be what you need.

WHAT'S YOUR BRAND VIBE?

Answer these questions to zero in on your brand vibe.

What is your brand's mission?

- What is your central vision for your brand? Three-month goals? Six-month goals? One-year goals?
- What do you want your brand's impact on your community to be?
- Why do people need your brand?
- What do you want people to say about your brand to their followers, friends, and family?

What is your brand identity/persona?

- What are your brand's core values? These are your uncompromising truths and guiding principles that express what you stand for and the primary driving force behind your brand, business, behaviors, and decisions.
- When making a decision, ask yourself, "Is this in alignment with my values?" (This will be critical when you choose to work with different brands and collaborations.)

What's your brand persona/brand vibe?

- Pick five words that immediately speak to and describe your brand.
- What can and will your brand offer its audience?
- What is your value proposition?

What are your brand visuals?

- Color palette?
- Fonts for graphics?
- Photo edit style?
- Video thumbnails?

CHAPTER 3

DEFINE YOUR AUDIENCE

"It's just fun to help people."

—MRBEAST

While the number one reason influencers fail is because they lack self-, niche-, and brand-clarity, the second major pitfall is an offshoot. Most influencers are not as successful as they could be because they do not *truly* understand their audience.

I often see people with great intentions and so much passion make superficial assumptions by drawing from personal experience. They just haven't developed the habit of tracking metrics and living for the data. When it comes to your audience, research is critical. Success as a micro influencer is about serving the needs of your community. You can only do that if you do know what your people want. So, break your niche audience down and consider the distinct profiles of the people you'd like to attract within that community.

Alongside your tribe, there are three other core groups to be constantly tuned into. Together, I call them the Core Four. Again, if you have done some of this work, stay with me; you likely haven't done it this way and there is likely more for you to learn.

THE CORE FOUR

You don't only have one audience; you have four to maintain. It may sound like a ton of work but it's not. Let me explain. Your Core Four are your:

1. Real audience
2. Ideal audience
3. Heroes
4. Niche-related allies

Let's start with Real Audience.

REAL AUDIENCE

Your Real Audience is made up of the people who follow you now or at any given moment. They are an essential group to evaluate constantly. Review your audience analytics today and two weeks from now, and make it a frequent practice.

If you have not yet been focused on curating a community around a specific niche and growing organically, your Instagram account will be a random collection of people. They will be old friends you had from school, strangers you swapped business cards with at the local Starbucks, and other random people who friended you on the platform because you seem cool. Within this group, you likely have a collection of the people you want more of—your Ideal Audience—and many people who don't fit the criteria.

Analyze your Real Audience. Who is following you at this moment? Go into your insights and find out what location is following you the most. If you live in New York City and most of your followers are from Malaysia or Europe (and you've never lived on another continent), you might have a handful of sketchy spammers in your group. Remember how ghost followers throw off engagement rates? Delete any strange accounts that seem spammy because they aren't active, have few followers, or seem like they have no reason to be following you. And don't take me the wrong way: one of the major benefits of social media is expanding your reach and making global friends. Legit people might be from either one of those places, but if the accounts look odd or you see a massive number of people from one area you have no connection to, that's weird.

Next, consider the gender and ages of the people who follow you. Gender is valuable information. If you are a new mommy influencer and your audience is 80 percent men, that needs to change. Age range is another critical metric to notice. If your audience is primarily people over fifty, once again you might be off-target as a new mommy blogger. Not saying a woman can't have a baby over the age of fifty—props to the oldest recorded mother to date, who was seventy-four!—but that is not the majority.

It's okay to make generalizations like this when they are based on stats. For instance, the Office for National Statistics reported that the number of births to women over fifty has quadrupled over the last two decades, up from fifty-five in 2001 to 238 in 2016. That is proof it's a very tiny group. Remember the niche down conversation from Chapter 2? This is a prime example of too narrow an audience.

After you analyze your insights, go through comments on your posts. Who is engaging the most? Again, you might see a mix of friends who fit what you think is your target audience, people you met once who still follow you, or maybe your mom. Shout out to the passionate, supportive family members who make the best cheerleaders.

Visit people's profiles. Especially the ones you think might be in your Ideal Audience. Get curious. Ask yourself these questions:

- What do they post?
- What do they like?
- What do they hate?
- What filters and colors do they use?
- How active are they on their platform?
- What products do they talk about or show in their pictures?
- When you click on the mega influencer accounts you follow, do you notice that these people also follow them?

Now, when you get clear on your niche and start posting on-brand content, members of your current Real Audience will likely unfollow you. Do not freak out. You have now defined your message, and these people may not be into it. They likely followed you once for a random reason or because you know them from childhood. Your auntie might stick by you through and through, but Sarah, who had been into pictures of your pug, might not love your new fashion vibe. Be okay with the unfollows. They are doing you a favor. You are posting targeted content and cleaning your list. You only want to keep people who want to be in your community and engage with it.

Never create a new account to segment your audience and start from scratch, even if you find out that only 5 percent are in your target demographic or you switch your niche. The Instagram algorithm has a history on you that might have nothing to do with the people following you. Since day one, Instagram has made assumptions based on data about who you follow, what you like, what profiles you view and engage with and seem interested in. When you create a new account, the algorithm doesn't know you. It's why the platform offers you a menu of famous Instagram accounts to follow, like The Rock and Kim Kardashian or *The Tonight Show*. When you shift niches or start seriously posting targeted content, the people you don't want will fall away, but the ones who are quality followers will stay connected and the algorithm's data on you will grow. So, do not start from scratch.

One remarkable aspect of being a micro influencer is that you can reinvent yourself a million times. If you went to college, how many majors were you into before you chose one? Or maybe you figured it out the first time, but you realize it's not what you want to do, so you changed. It's easier to pivot like that on social media. You can change your niche whenever what you are doing doesn't resonate.

Again, people will unfollow you, but that's okay because you are flipping the script. Just avoid posting some weird Instagram filter on a photo of your dog, then the new couch you just got, and then tacos. Who are you? That kind of content doesn't make it very clear.

You *want* unengaged people to peace out. In the end, it's about high engagement rates. Brands do care how many followers you have to a certain degree, but if you only have six thousand followers and a solid, engaged following, you can still make money. Both Instagram and brands care more about that and less about your follower count. Hence the title micro influencer. Who cares if five hundred people unfollow you if they didn't engage with your account at all? *Thank you*, you should say when they leave. They were messing up your engagement rate.

You also might see people who follow you engage with you more than you expected or start talking about you once you start posting more niche-related targeted content. It goes both ways. Either way, you'll be cleaning house and honing in on your Ideal Audience.

IDEAL AUDIENCE

Your Ideal Audience are the people you want to have follow you. Your goal is to find a narrow audience interested in one topic where you also hold a deep interest. Again, if you don't give a shit about your niche topic, authenticity and sincerity become hard to sell, which is crucial to your growth. So make sure you give a damn about what you choose.

Of course, you also need to make sure that their audience-backed interest is recognized by Instagram. People must be searching for the topic you want to discuss. Before spending hours on content vision boards, plans, and snapping shots, make sure there is an audience. Are there like-minded accounts, all of which you can quickly discover through a simple hashtag search?

Remember, if you build a broad brand, you'll have a broad audience and brands won't want to work with you. If you're a fitness influencer, for example, there are millions of you. What sets you apart? Find your target audience in that niche. Workout routines made for the busy entrepreneur? Yoga for jocks? (By the way, joga is a thing.) Or maybe you're a vegan queen.

Especially in growth mode, proper segmentation is critical to your success. If you only have a couple hundred or a few thousand followers, they might not be your ideal target, and that's okay, but you need to make that distinction. Categorize your current followers into groups to separate your Real Audience from the Ideal Audience you currently have. Here are the questions to ask:

- Age
- Gender
- Location
- Occupation
- How do they define themselves? Labels they use?
- What do they repost?
- What results do they want?
- What solutions can you offer?
- What do they want to experience?

- What accounts do they follow? What are the categories of those accounts?
- What hashtags do they use?
- Where do they go? What geolocations do they tag?
- What brands do they post about?

Understand the psychology of your Ideal Audience. Everyone on the internet is looking out for *me*. They aren't going to care about you because you want them to. So, why do they use Instagram? Find out, then capitalize on what that is. The more you know about your Ideal Audience, the more likely you'll be able to provide laser-focused content that serves their needs and implement the proper strategy for growth. Ideally, you want more Ideals to become the Reals.

Most people use social media as a means of escape and inspiration. Generally, you want to keep your account positive. Become their go-to person. Be a source of escape, inspiration, education, and understanding for your Ideal Audience.

Outside of your research, conduct surveys in your network. It's a great way to engage. You can easily find if your current ideal people are aligned with your vision through simple surveys and polls. Ask questions with stories. Then, document the data. Keep a record of it all. If 64 percent of your audience is interested in the most durable dog toys, that will be helpful as you decide what brands you want to reach out to. Gauge their interests. To make it easier, ask your followers questions like:

- What kind of content do you want to see more of from me?
- What's the number one _____ (niche-related category of item) you cannot live without?

- What's your favorite brand? Give them three to four options.
- What's one thing you wish you had more time for?

Gathering information like this is also one way to overwhelm potential brand partners with relevant data in your portfolio, which we will discuss later.

Engage your audience for feedback at least once a month to keep your data up to date as you grow. You might need to incentivize people to participate by offering a prize like a personal shout-out, a gift card, or an enticing lead magnet. Think about some questions that are relevant to your niche, write them down, and place them in your calendar to remember to ask them. Always split test long-form responses against quick responses. People respond differently in every market, so it is imperative to define your Ideal Audience clearly.

Your Ideal Audience will also be the most engaged segment of your Hero Accounts, which are the accounts you look up to. We'll cover them next.

HEROES

Hero accounts are the profiles within your niche you aspire to emulate. They tend to be macro influencers and mega influencers or even seasoned micro influencers you can tell are crushing the game. They are the accounts you follow and aspire to be. They are your competitors, per se. They may even be people you might be jealous of. If you are irritated by another influencer's success, it's a cue that you wish you had the same level of influence they do. Put your ego aside and follow them. You can learn a lot by watching. Identify what they are doing better or their missed opportunities (that you could fill), and start to understand the people who follow them.

Find one hundred of these Hero accounts that align with your niche, brand, and audience to scale over time consistently. If you can't find one hundred, don't stress—but do spend time finding as many as you can. One hundred accounts sounds like a lot, but it isn't. It will take some effort, but it's worth it, 100 percent.

Once you have your Heroes, find out what they are posting that people are engaging with the most. Go through the comments and click on their followers' profiles. You will see trends. Maybe you see moms with toddlers. Or couples who care about traveling. Or environmentally conscious people.

The intel you gain will offer you clues about the Ideal Audience you share and what those people care about. You'll be able to connect the dots and categorize them: The mommy blogger. The digital nomad entrepreneur. The vintage clothing shopper. You might see new trends emerge. You might see couples randomly following more travel accounts because they're looking for their honeymoon place. Focus most on people who are more engaged. They are the ones who like a post, even if it was an emoji. Here are some questions to help you understand the people following your Heroes:

- What are their interests?
- What do they post?
- What are their lives like?

- What do they seem to care about?
- What do they bitch about?
- What makes them happy?

Focus on what people are passionate about but also their complaints. People rant on social media about their issues. It's incredible because, though you're no therapist (unless you are), you can be a source of motivation by sharing about a similar personal experience or by sharing a simple quote that makes you smile. You can be the one to solve their problem. Motivational accounts typically do very well on social media because people always search for a sense of community. They want to know they aren't alone or the only frustrated person. They want to know that they are not the only people who have bad days.

Study your Heroes. Invest time into learning about your competition so you can continually refine and grow. Sign up for their email lists. Follow all of them! Turn their post notifications on. Follow these related accounts to see what they offer. What are their unique selling points and propositions? What kind of content do they share regularly? What are they doing that you are not? Pride yourself in being different, but also humbly learn. If it's working for them now, it can work for you.

Once you have at least fifteen to twenty Heroes on a list, pick your top five. Your Hero 5 are the competitors most aligned with your brand. Pick the accounts that appear to have almost everything, if not everything you want. Then do a thorough competitor analysis on them. Audit their accounts and define their strengths and weaknesses and the key takeaways from each you wish to implement on your account.

Find your competition's general audience's age range, sex, geographical location, predominant race, job, earnings, aesthetic, and other top accounts they follow. An easy way to do this is to pull Nitreo or HypeAuditor analyses (those are two great platforms to Google) for your Heroes. Then define why you are different and unique from your Hero 5 as well as your similarities.

Don't overwhelm yourself completely. You could spend a year on this, but you don't want to. Pick your Hero 5; go through their top six posts. Look at the comments and document what you see. Make this a frequent practice. Use the chart at the end of this chapter that was created to make this easy for you.

While your Hero 100 is "competition," remember you are working towards helping people in your niche. They are your teammates. You've got your family to feed, yourself to feed, and your life to live—it is about your business, but it doesn't hurt to make these people your friends. You might even reach out. Send a DM saying, *We might be trying to get the same partnerships, but dude, I love what you're doing!*

There are also your niche-related allies. And they are great to partner with too. Team up with them and together you can grow faster.

NICHE-RELATED ALLIES

Your niche-related allies are the accounts that are within your vertical but don't offer the same content focus as you. For example, let's say you're a photographer with an international travel niche. Niche-related allies would be travel videographers, travel bloggers, and hotel bloggers. These are people you could collaborate with and build an online network with. They are accounts that have a community that is likely to engage with your brand as well because you share the same content vertical.

No one is you, and that's the beauty of social media. You're going to hundreds of influencers *like* you, but you'll never be them and they will never be you. You'll each motivate the same audience in a completely different way. So keep your cool and think abundantly. Understanding them, making friends, and knowing how they work will help you be a better influence.

I have seen influencers go crazy stressing about where they are compared to other influencers in their space. You can easily transcend any negative vibes by surrendering to where you are; respecting the day-to-day process, setting weekly, monthly, and quarterly goals for your influencer journey; and placing emphasis on serving your community. When you have clarity on where you want to go and you know you're down to commit to whatever it takes to get there, the sky honestly is limited. Also, think about how you can help others too. You'll get further faster with this mindset.

I've encountered a couple Instagram coaches who have threatened me and messaged me all insecure about me chatting with some of their followers. Honestly I was shocked by their haste. First, I would never even think to do such a thing. Second, they didn't know me. Plus, they don't own the platform and their followers.

But then I remembered how the most successful influencers

and entrepreneurs I know truly live a life of abundance. Their followers are not just a number, or a dollar sign; they know there is *always* enough community to go around.

We are all in this together, here to serve one another, here to make money together. This is why I live and do business by megaentrepreneur and author of *Connected to Goodness*, David Meltzer's, motto: my daily goal is to help a lot of people, make a lot of money, and have a lot of fun.

When abundance is your foundation, you show you are secure in what you have to offer the world. People resonate with that. It's impossible to not win with that mentality. Not to mention, you won't drive yourself crazy or seriously compromise your business by getting your ego in the way.

COMPETITIVE ANALYSIS REVEALS YOUR BRAND POWER

You must regularly enter the day-to-day conversation already taking place in the minds of your followers and potential followers, your brand partners, and your Heroes. What are their greatest frustrations, challenges, dreams, and desires? What motivates them? Click on the top commenter profiles for your Heroes. What are their most significant priorities on the platform? It is your job to create intrigue among your audience, and you can't effectively do that if you don't understand their psychology. You will soon learn you must wear different hats for different audiences because everyone is not the same.

Generally, people follow and interact with an influencer for one of two reasons:

1. For a logical, analytical, informative connection
2. For an emotional/inspirational connection

How do you serve both people with your content? By keeping a healthy balance of information and emotional and inspirational connection. And always post with this mentality: offer value over personal gain.

Become obsessed with how to serve your audience. How do I provide value in the ways they best receive it? You have to give them a no-brainer offer that makes that half-second decision to follow you easy. You want them to think, *Of course I'll follow. Your feed is dope! Of course I'll engage with you! This person knows what I want to see and read on Instagram.*

When you tune in and track, you will notice small nuances that become the keys that unlock your success. For example, I once used to think people followed me because they wanted me to show them strategies for how to make money online. By tracking audience analytics, I learned what they want from me is slightly different than what I first thought. They are seeking the motivation to make more money. I wouldn't have known that had I not taken the time to understand who follows me. I would have made generalizations, continued to post moneymaking strategies only, and missed an opportunity to provide more value and build a committed and vibrant community.

Ultimately, the connection you have with your audience is why any big brand wants to work with you. The simplest way to always do this is to ask the question: how do I serve? Coming from that place also makes what you are doing easier in a way. It's less of a struggle, less about the number of people, and less about stressing over the fact you aren't where you want to be or that you have to come up with a clever post again.

In most areas of life, when it's less about you, it's more about you in the end. I have learned that the less I focus on myself, the more I focus on helping people, the more money and connections I make—and it's more enjoyable. Why it works like that, I don't know. Plus, it's human nature to a degree to be of service, especially when our needs are met. We are meant to be in a community. When we are connected, it's not natural to be focused solely on ourselves. That would be weird. When you're helping other people, you're helping yourself, and when you're becoming a better expert, you're winning because you are learning and sharing what people need to know.

Serving others can force you to learn too. I work with a lot of micro influencers who think they haven't learned enough to be an authority. You have Google. You have cell phones. You have the internet anywhere in the world. Learn from someone, then teach that knowledge. It's easy to make any expert seem bigger than you. But it's not true. That expert learned from another expert, and you're going to do the same. An expert is someone who is continuously learning everything about a topic. If you can be that to people, you're so valuable to them. And if you're valuable to followers, you're needed by brands.

Prospecting on an ad platform nowadays is damn expensive. The micro influencer business is thriving because it allows brands to get in front of more eyes more efficiently and for less. The biggest complaint brands make all the time is they don't know how to find the influencers they need. With 37.8 million out there, it's overwhelming. If you're the right person for a brand and you're doing your research, you reach out, you get them.

So track, track, track your analytics. If you create a business or creator account within Instagram, you can review your insights. Do a simple Google search to dive into your analytics further. What's the likely gross income of the people who follow you based on age and location? Click into a decent amount of follower profiles. What are they into? What places do they go? What products do they use? What hashtags do they like? What stage of life are they in? Be smart about your audience, messaging, and positioning, and lastly, have a great bio.

BIO PRECISION

Once you know the audience you want to attract, you know your brand positioning, and you have a solid understanding of Instagram's rules, regulations, and reward system, you can begin optimizing your account for growth. That always begins with your bio.

A good bio has to be simple, precise, and actionable. People should immediately understand what you're about when they click your profile and what they will receive if they follow you. Your bio should also evoke curiosity. It should inspire people to want to know more about your content. Your bio has to sell you on the spot. Most users only take a few seconds to scan a bio and photos before deciding whether or not they should follow. It's why knowing your brand proposition is so crucial.

An engaging bio has four components:

1. A description of you
2. Your brand value proposition
3. Your contact information
4. A strong call to action

Write one sentence for each of the above components and that is your bio. Now, you might already have done this work. However, what I find with many influencers is that they need to tweak once they review these components. Do an audit on your bio to make sure you have all four.

A DESCRIPTION OF YOU

The best Instagram bios include a clear self-description and brand value proposition. It should include your job title or the name of the company you own, claims to fame, and what makes you stand out.

My bio clearly states that I am an influencer growth coach. I also add my wins to show I know what I am talking about. In my bio, as of writing this book, it says $150M+ in revenue. People who find me immediately know what I do and that I have a proven track record.

YOUR BRAND VALUE PROPOSITION

People need to understand the specific verticals your account focuses on—for example, nature photographer, mental health advocate, LA foodie. Here's mine: I help influencers grow and monetize their channels. It's to the point and straightforward.

YOUR CONTACT INFORMATION

Provide your contact email so that brands know exactly where to reach you. It seems obvious, but you'd be surprised how many people don't do it. Be sure that you take advantage of all the information Instagram allows you to share in your bio. Add your email to your profile so brands can easily click the email CTA.

A STRONG CALL TO ACTION

Direct people to take action. Tell them precisely what you want them to do. You will increase the number of engaged followers you gain dramatically by having a clear call to action (CTA).

The best call to action is to take advantage of the link box. You can direct people to subscribe to your blog, or send traffic to a link tree, a YouTube video, your website, and your email subscription lead form. Gary Vee has a great CTA. He asks followers to text him and then he lists a number where anyone can contact him. A great CTA is always "DM me," and then you insert a specific keyword and request something like, "Mention code FALL FAVS to get a list of my favorite fall products."

Make sure you have a Google Analytics account set up on your site if you are linking off of Instagram. Always place a

Google Urchin Tracking Module (UTM) code on your page so you can quickly analyze the success of your CTA. UTM codes are phrases added to the end of a site URL that help you track the source of the website traffic.

If you're struggling with your bio, don't guess. Grab your Hero 20 list. Copy and paste their profile bios into a document. Put them into a word cloud generator and find the most common keywords and be sure to use the exact relative keywords in your bio.

Having an optimized bio is not only crucial for expressing who you are with the world and attracting your ideal followers, but it's also important because of the Instagram search optimization feature. You need to be found. Instagram's search engine ranks the best accounts using the Topical Authorities feature in Instagram. A topical authority is a profile Instagram has logged as an established expert over an entire topic instead of one hashtag.

The best way to think about a topical authority is to look at niches within a topic. Take the topic of low-carb diets, for instance. There are a lot of possible ideas and concepts floating around that core category. You might consider using a hashtag in your bio like #lowcarbrecipes as a niche related to the larger topic of #lowcarbdiet so your bio is retrieved when users search that hashtag. But Instagram doesn't make links the same way that we do. The hashtag #lowcarbrecipes might seem similar to #weightlossdiet, but they aren't the same to Instagram. The algorithm wouldn't recommend low-carb diet recipes to someone interested in muscle building and losing weight.

Instagram provides recommendations to its users, from hashtags to content to who they might want to follow. They determine what recommendations they should follow based on the interests of the users on their platform. They do this by using a formula that considers topical authorities. So, if you were a follower of @fentybeauty, @jamescharles, and @urbandecay, who all post makeup or beauty-related content, Instagram will determine that you are interested in the topic of makeup or beauty.

When Instagram does this, they also take into consideration the hashtag groups you use. They group the hashtags you might put in your comments or captions and assign them to specific topics. So, if you used the hashtag #euphoriamakeup in a post, they may assign this to the topic of makeup, which helps them determine that you are a topical authority on makeup. Suppose it decides you are, in fact, a topical authority on makeup. In that case, people who are interested in that topic will discover your content through hashtag feeds, explore pages, and recommended accounts.

It's imperative you use the specific keywords relative to your niche within your bio so that you can be shown to others. And it sets you apart from the influencers who want to be paid to be hot because what keywords are they using other than weird-ass emojis? I run into a lot of people who say, "I'm not a model. I'm an influencer." What does that mean? Brands don't want to work with people who are not clearly defined, because they want to run targeted ads. If a brand doesn't know who your audience is, your platform is not useful for them. So, immediately when you describe yourself, show your audience that you post with intention. Hashtag your niche within your larger niche and make sure that people are looking for it.

Positions of status, affiliations, and titles also need to be on-brand for them to make sense in your bio. Professional clout is excellent, but make sure you're doing it right. An instance where it would hurt you is if you are a fashion influencer who posts clothes, but you are also a Skinny Mint Tea Ambassador and use that affiliation in your bio. That's not helpful to any fashion brand because it's not their audience and doesn't do anything for you. You're telling people you're all about weight loss while they are about fashion. On the other hand, if it's related to your niche, go for it.

Don't bend the truth, either. People have asked me if they can say they are ambassadors for Nike. My answer is always, *Are you a recognized ambassador for Nike? Does the company see you as one?* If the answer is no, which it often is, don't stretch the truth to say sporting Nike 24/7 means you're an ambassador. Do feature affiliations you have established and anywhere you've been published.

When I started with my agency, I split tested all types of hashtags and statements to gain bio precision. I once used to link to major influencers that I had worked with so that other management companies and labels would know that I had a proven track record. Affiliations that give you authority within a particular space are always helpful, especially when you are building a reputation. I have done over $150 million in revenue for brands, which is in my bio because it validates that I know what I am doing.

If you don't have affiliations to brag about yet, don't worry. Focus on serving your audiences, and brands will look at this to see if they should dig deeper into your analytics and see if they are aligned with what you're trying to achieve.

Once your bio is solid, your job will be to always post epic content. So the next chapter is about post quality, story content, captions, and the feed aesthetic needed for accelerated account growth.

DO THIS NOW:

- Analyze your Real Audience. Who is following you? Where are they from? What age groups? How many fit your Ideal Audience?
- Narrow in on your Ideal Audience. To do this, you might first do research on your Hero accounts. Begin building avatars for your Ideal Audience. Who do you want to serve?
- Create a spreadsheet to analyze your Hero 100 similar to the template shown below. Narrow the list down to your Hero 5. What did you learn by doing this work?
- Nail your bio. Does your bio follow the rules for bio precision? Do an audit.

Top Hero Organizational Chart

IG Handle	ER %	Followers #	Notifications on?	Specific Niche	IG Bio	List Recent Brand Deals	Left two cents on recent posts?	Engaged with TOP commenters on posts?	Engaged with TOP commenters' personal posts?	Engaged with TOP commenters' personal stories?

CHAPTER 4

CREATE EPIC CONTENT

"I stay true to myself and my style, and I am always pushing myself to be aware of that and be original."

—AALIYAH

With over 37.8 million micro influencers you have to stand out. If you have decided, in your heart, that you are going for this *for real*—you plan to make this a job where you get paid—then you must invest in your craft.

You are here to serve. Always remember that. As often as possible, provide value to your audience because that is how you scale and how Instagram rates you as follow-worthy. Your job as an influencer is to be helpful, needed, and worth following. Quality content has little to do with personal opinion. It checks the box on these two variables:

1. Aesthetic
2. Relevance

When people consider what high-quality content is, they often first think about professional-looking photos. While photos taken with higher-quality lenses are crucial, much more is required to create high-quality content as rated by Instagram's algorithm. While you do need to create visually appealing content and align with the vibe of your brand and audience, you also have to provide value. Your content has to teach people or be entertaining or inspiring in some capacity. Ideally, it's all three.

The beauty is when you start mastering content, you'll find that you can't be anyone but yourself. You become more self-expressed on the platform, which might translate to more confidence overall in life. And since there is no one like you, you might as well master sharing that with the world. In this chapter you will learn evergreen marketing principles that will make you a master of captivating content.

While you probably have a good sense of what your audience likes, again, I say, don't skip this chapter. You will likely get a deeper understanding here, which will ultimately help you earn more money. Remember that foundation and engagement are critical to your ability to skyrocket your following and offer quality content, and that is how you land brand deals. The reality is, brands will not work with you if all those aspects aren't on point.

INSTAGRAM CREATIVE

There are four rules to creating epic content that your audience loves. The rules apply to all platforms but because there are slight variations between them, this chapter focuses on Instagram and includes sections on TikTok and YouTube.

Since our primary focus is Instagram, we will start there. Here are the principles you must follow to succeed as an influencer:

1. Ace aesthetics
2. Consistency is king
3. Invoke FOMO

Similar rules apply to TikTok and YouTube, but I will address the slight nuances of working with those platforms separately. So, let's start with aesthetic appeal and how to look good online, and specifically on Instagram.

ACE AESTHETICS

Instagram is a visual platform where eye-catching content wins. Find your look, your vibe, and then stick with what you decide. Do you prefer warmer tones? Or cooler images? Black-and-white photography? Factor in what you learned when you explored the profiles of your Heroes. Whatever your editing style, make sure it's consistent so your posts flow within your feed. Even adding a touch of the same filter each time you post can make your feed more cohesive. Also, all of your photos, graphics, and videos must be high resolution, crisp, and clear. Use good lighting and pops of color. Face shots perform best. Avoid dim light and shadows.

I have learned from my model friends that it pays to practice in the mirror. You might feel awkward, but that's normal. Take numerous photos of your poses and decide, *Do I like this? Is this the look I am going for?* Almost everyone feels strange taking photos or speaking to a camera. Don't stress it—practice! Your most high-converting poses will naturally start coming to you. Also, when in doubt, go to YouTube. If you want to model better there are tutorials on YouTube. Learn poses there like how to look into the camera, or pose naturally, or pose with products. Start creating collections of Instagram poses you like that other influencers look good doing. And you will learn through split testing different photos what your audience responds to most.

Invest in a decent tripod too. It will be your best friend. Not everyone can have a photographer around all of the time, and you don't want to wait for your next meetup with a professional to produce content, or for your roommate to get home, or to bug your partner again. You're a content creator who always wants to be in high demand. Be ready to produce quality content on the go. Whether you're using an iPhone, an Android phone, a DSLR camera, or a $10,000 camera, invest in a tripod.

Now, some influencers make money shooting on iPhones, but there is so much competition. If you are serious, buy a good camera. It will help you stand out and look professional. If you scroll into a photo, you can see how pixelated it is when it's been taken with an iPhone. Many companies have issues with these shots. High-resolution photos are professional, so that is what you want. Brands are looking for clear, stunning images of their beautiful products. No one will pay for a shitty resolution.

People should be able to tell the difference in the quality of content from free to paid content. There's UGC that large corporations get from customers for free, and then there's UGC that brands can get from influencers for a price. If you're shooting on an iPhone and they're getting customer reviews that are also on an iPhone, they could pay you lower amounts since it doesn't stand out from what they're already getting. Position yourself so that your content is quality and you can demand more for it. If a brand wants to pay you fifty dollars for a post, you can negotiate more if you shoot on a Canon and take time to edit.

Also, go back to your Hero accounts again. Identify the posts they have with the most engagement from the past three months. Do you notice any similarities in angles, lighting, or color? You can learn a lot about what visuals work in your niche by pulling from what they're doing.

Instagram analyzes your photos. Certain angles might better articulate what is occurring in a particular image. The better the angle, the more likely Instagram will promote it to the appropriate people. When you take photos, play. Test angles. Try the various editing features. Test how close or far you are from people. Manipulating these variables can help Instagram accurately depict what's going on in your photo. That said, you want to also be consistent with your visuals.

CONSISTENCY IS KING

Be consistent. Brands want to work with value-based influencers. You must frequently post, along with aesthetic streamlining that you maintain with standard colors and visually stunning images.

Anyone who comes to your platform should immediately get a sense of who you are. Immediately they should grasp that your profile was created to provide value to a specific target audience. Representatives of brands, most specifically, require this. They want assurance that featuring their products will provide value and feel natural to your feed.

Instagram favors original, topic-specific content. Random accounts are tough to grow, because Instagram was designed to share your life with the world. Don't throw the algorithm off. The algorithm connects you with like-minded people. Don't fight it. Always make your message clear.

Define your specific content strategy. You can't be posting cats, then memes, then a picture of a tree, when you want to grow with intent. Your account will go into the algorithm's *Nah, Bro* realm. It will not be shown to more people. Content must be aligned to one prominent topic like international travel, Palm Springs vibes, or basketball tricks. Get specific, so when it comes time to promote products and monetize your account, your followers will respond. Consistent, high-quality content is how you grow engagement. People will want to follow you because if they don't, they could be missing out on something valuable.

ENVOKE FOMO (FEAR OF MISSING OUT)

Evoking FOMO is not possible if you do not understand your audience. What do they want to see? If you know your audience, you will understand what they want and need. Maybe they want to make more money online—then, your account needs to talk about how to make more money. If you're a foodie, maybe the people who follow you want to see the food they've never seen before or the local hot spots at which to dine, or your latest healthy, delicious meal. How do you inspire them to eat, or cook, or visit these places?

Your goal is to have people aspire to be better in some way. You don't always need to make people feel good, though it is one useful strategy. The idea is to create leverage. They should look at your posts and think:

"Man, I wish I had…"

"I wish I could go there!"

"I wish I could go do that."

"I should pursue that."

"I wish I could create that."

You have to build an "I look up to you just as much as I relate to you" connection with your audience. You need also to invoke this feeling with representatives of brands. You are always creating the "I wish we worked with this person" feeling.

In general, Instagram accounts that make people feel good or offer growth opportunities are the most successful. Focus on speaking to people about the four innate human needs. They are:

1. Money
2. Food
3. Relationships
4. Status

If you can inspire an action related to those verticals, you win. Be aware that accounts that focus on negativity don't do as well. And if they do, they have a short fuse, because people want to feel happy. People do not go on Instagram to get bummed out. When people say they need an Instagram break, it's because there's too much comparison, they're feeling like they aren't good enough, or there's no happiness in their feed. So the more you can be a positive light to people, the more engagement you should get on your account.

Lastly, is what you are posting timely or relevant to what's happening now? Stay in the loop on your scoop. When you go through the trouble of producing your high-quality content, ensure it's topical and, most importantly, well within your niche. How relevant is your content to what's popular now? How relevant is it to what is thoroughly engaged with on the platform? One of the best ways to organically feature yourself and become top of mind to a brand and community is to tag the companies and people in the photos and videos you post.

Always leave a CTA on your posts. What do you want them to do next? Answer a question? Describe a related experience? Click the link in your bio? Save your post? Direct your audience to create a quality content experience. These rules apply to all platforms all the time, especially Instagram.

But let's also address TikTok, because you might be on it too.

TIKTOK CREATIVE

I'm not one to preach or tell people to do anything one specific way because it always boils down to *your* goal. But as an influencer who wants to make as significant an impact as possible and grow fast, you should get on TikTok.

Too many influencers say they don't want to take advantage of TikTok because it doesn't fit their personality. If that is you, I beg you to elevate your thinking. TikTok is a great space to share educational, inspirational, DIY tutorials, and comedic content. Over 1.5 billion users have downloaded the app. One video that goes viral on TikTok can lead to worldwide visibility. You can make it work for the followers you want to attract.

You can talk shit about TikTok all day (and I don't love to consume on the platform personally), but people on TikTok are killing it. Many creators have changed their lives and brand partnership opportunities seemingly overnight due to TikTok.

Charlie D'Amelio is a sixteen-year-old social media personality who made it big on the internet by posting dancing videos on the TikTok app. Currently her TikTok account has a massive following in the millions and she has a purported net worth of over $12 million.

It's like the beginning phases of Instagram all over again. The hype is real. Take advantage. Brands are already crazy about it. If you don't want to, that's fine, but you might be limiting your pool of opportunities. How bad do you want this? Get on there and follow fifteen to twenty niche hashtags pronto.

TikTok is a platform where staying on top of trends will help you succeed. Know what is going viral and produce your creative remixes or inspiration for those trends quickly. Be smart and take care of your Reel and TikTok content at the same time by saving it before pushing it live (to avoid the watermark).

Daily posting is the key to success on TikTok. You have to post much more than other platforms—at least every day, three times a day. Some people post ten times a day, which is why many influencers don't want to bother. The goal is to figure out what works for you. Remember, these are very short videos. They do require some editing, so schedule a bit more time in your day. And if you're creating Reels, you should be doing TikToks.

Landing on the For You page (FYP) should be your continuous goal because users see this when they first open the app. You don't have to have a lot of followers to do it, either. The FYP provides a significant opportunity to increase your engagement rate and reach new niche-related members of your community—brands and fans alike.

The For You page is very targeted and curated to each users' interests. The algorithm continuously learns you by tracking the videos you engage with, hashtags you follow, your location and language preferences, and the type of content you create. Then, it serves you related content. Stepping up your hashtag game is an excellent way to on this page. Hashtags are essential for TikTok growth. You need to follow fifteen to twenty niche hashtags, regularly analyze their posts and engagement rates, and interact daily with the most recent videos. When you post on TikTok, use a combination of trending hashtags on the discover page. Commit regular time to learning what is popping on the platform. Core hashtags are

#viral #fyp #trending. Also, use niche-specific hashtags that are very specific to what you are posting.

Avoid using more than seven hashtags per post. Always switch them up too, so that it stays relevant. Aim for two megahashtags, two smaller core hashtags, and two niche-related hashtags. Also, make sure the hashtags have good viewership—tens to hundreds of millions behind them, just like Instagram. Hashtags with minimal usage will not help you get discovered. Use hashtags with millions, hundreds of millions, or billions whenever possible. And split test everything. That is the beauty of posting numerous times per day. You get to quickly see what works and what does not.

Always post for the best time for your current time zone, not when you feel your followers are hanging out late at night. I can't tell you how many people hit me up saying, *I just posted and it's tanking,* but it was at 2:00 a.m. While there are night owls who scroll late, they're a small percentage. They also don't have high intent. Think about when you're on social media because you can't sleep. You're not engaged. Instead, you're mindlessly scrolling and liking. So, when is your audience actively engaged? When are they hanging out on social media?

Under Manage Account in User Settings, switch to a Pro Account. This will give you an understanding of your audience insights, including your most active and engaged days and hours. Use Instagram best practices here too. Don't shoot in shitty lighting. You won't go viral. Also, always be quick on TikTok trends. Add trending music or sound bites. Stick to your niche. Don't forget the headlines and captions. And, tell a story whenever possible.

To get as much of your content on the For You page as possible, engage with your community and niche hashtags thirty minutes before you post and thirty minutes to one hour later. Reply to every comment under your video. Take advantage of the vast array of growth opportunities on TikTok, post valuable or entertaining content consistently, and you won't be disappointed. The same applies to YouTube.

YOUTUBE CONTENT

During the creation of this book, I interviewed a group of very successful YouTube influencers. When I asked them if they had any special growth techniques to share, the consensus was in line with what most influencers say and what we've already covered. It was to: (1) post consistently and (2) be yourself and always showcase what makes you unique.

All the content rules you've learned thus far apply to YouTube, but there is one small nuance on that platform that will set you apart and is easily missed. If you want to make more money (and we'll talk more about YouTube monetization in Chapters 6 and 7) make better thumbnails.

On YouTube, the thumbnail is a pivotal content component because it is what will entice or repel a viewer to click and watch your video. It's as important as a headline on an ad, a magazine cover that makes you want to buy, or a trailer for a movie.

Popular American YouTuber MrBeast, whose content is designed around expensive stunts, once said he would pay a graphic designer as much as $10,000 to design a thumbnail because it earned him even more. Compelling thumbnails have three components. They have:

1. **Consistent branding.** The primary background color is consistent with the channel. The same goes for secondary colors and fonts.
2. **A captivating headline.** Thumbnails should have a title and related text where words clearly stand out from the background image. The language must clearly communicate what the video is about. Sans serif is a standard font style for thumbnails.
3. **Show off your personality.** Expressive faces do better. Also, add images that correlate to your niche. If you use a picture of yourself, don't pull it out of the video. Use a high-resolution image.

Avoid clickbait. It affects the algorithm negatively and pisses off viewers. Also, check your metrics regularly to make sure your thumbnails are working. If one isn't, change it. When in doubt, use a thumbnail maker or go to Canva for a thumbnail template.

YouTuber Alexandra Stewart of the show *After the Island* @ aftertheisland also suggests hosting live chats and premieres to amp up engagement. You can interact with your audience in real-time as a video launches. For her show, she went live every single day on YouTube while *Love Island USA* was airing. "The live chat was the best part about it because you have your own little group that has inside jokes...it becomes more of a family where the audience truly cares." She said connecting with your audience can be what makes you (or breaks you if you don't).

Javi Luna, who is an actor, singer, model, and social influencer with over 12 million followers on his social media platforms, says one clever way to engage is to include the audience as a part of videos just as if they were there. For example, a challenge where you don't know an event is taking place on screen but the audience does creates an inclusive environment.

What about length of video for YouTube content? YouTubers tend to have different perspectives and it makes sense because it comes down to niche and audience. Fashion and beauty YouTuber Angela Babicz @angelababicz says when it comes to vlogs, the longer the better. "Humans are nosy and want to know what everyone else is doing," she said.

Though, she also pointed out that tutorials and sponsored content are best kept short and to the point. It makes sense because for how-to videos, what people want most are the steps so they can get in action right away. And Stewart pointed out that interviews tend to be better if they are longer videos.

When it comes to quality content, small nuances make a difference and so does knowing your audience. Track analytics. Tweak your strategy if it's not working, and always make sure you are following overall best practices for epic content.

OVERALL BEST PRACTICES FOR EPIC CONTENT

As a micro influencer, the majority of your day-to-day work is to create content for your community. And that content must stand out if you plan to be a success and score brand deals. That requires being strategic, thinking ahead, and tracking what works. You must:

- Diversify through verticals
- Plan ahead
- Streamline feed aesthetic
- Create savable content
- Keep your caption game strong
- Post frequently
- Track your metrics
- Steer clear of content block

Once you do all that, you will be an epic content creator.

DIVERSIFY THROUGH VERTICALS

First, define your content macro vertical and the possible micro verticals and nano verticals you can speak to within those. I have included a worksheet for you to thoroughly plan this outlink at the end of this chapter. There are three verticals to break content into:

- Macro Vertical—Major Category
- Micro Vertical—Subcategory
- Nano Verticals—Smaller categories within a subcategory

Suppose you're a travel influencer like Sabrina Ross @with. love.brina. She is an exploration fanatic who lives to get lost in all the beautiful places this magnificent world has to offer. She had to travel for work so she started posting on Instagram and people started DMing her asking questions about the places she'd been and her favorite travel experiences. She decided to commit to creating a space where anyone in her network could come for travel inspiration and community. She now runs a very successful influencer business.

Travel is Sabrina's macro vertical. The places she goes are her micro categories. Suppose she jets over to Italy. She can break the city down into nano categories, which would be what travelers think about before traveling to another country or city. Nano categories for Venice, Italy, might be food, hotels, activities, and major attractions.

Organizing your content with verticals ensures you never run out and always keep it fresh. Choose seven to ten. Planning your content this way is easy. You can find a focus per week or month this way.

Stay on trend by searching trends outside of particular social media platforms. Use tools like Google Trends. If you're not familiar, Google Trends is a search feature that shows how frequently a given search term is entered into Google's search engine relative to the site's total search volume over a given period. Search Google trends relevant to your niche to help you define all of your verticals.

For example, say you're a fitness influencer, and you type in the term "fitness." It will give you all trends on the fitness macro vertical. It will also show you geographical areas where the term is being searched the most and provide the relevant search terms. Once you see a relevant trending topic, you can include it in your next post. Or, if you type in "fitness shoes" and see that a particular brand is trending, you should consider ordering your next pair from that brand and ride that trend. Google Trends is an effective way of knowing what's popular at any given moment within your niche.

If you want to grow into an influencer who is rewarded and

praised by brands, stop viewing your social media as everyone else does. Embody the fact that you are a content creator, not just an average Instagram user. Content diversification is critical, and defining your content verticals is how you diversify. Add a healthy mix of different angles when posting photos of yourself—full-length body shots, lifestyle product shots, various rooms and parts of your indoor shooting location, and outdoor shots (if it feels on-brand for you). You can't simply post selfies. Take advantage of shooting video content as often as you can: Reels, IGTVs, stories, and feed video posts on both Instagram and TikTok.

Instagram and TikTok are the masters of testing. When you post, the algorithm tests your content. It will show your post to a certain number of people, and if it does well, it will broaden that pool and show it to more people. Most people don't know that Instagram and TikTok thoroughly analyze the people reacting to your content. They will always promote your content to the particular niche that triggers activity. Anytime you post to Instagram, it looks for people who have similarities with the kinds of people who engage with your content. So, if they find that the majority of people who tap the "like" button on your photo are women, they will promote your photo to more women. If it is viewed and liked by more eighteen-year-olds, it will be promoted to those users.

Social media is a place for your brand, created to serve your audience. If you only post stories about yourself and never bother to acknowledge or ask your audience for feedback, you never really have any verifiable data to help expand your growth. Ultimately over time, your audience may lose interest. I have seen this time and time again with macro influencers. They stop engaging their audience for their needs and continue to keep doing what's worked in the past, and they begin to lose masses of followers because of it. You always have to be ready and willing to evolve by strategy and plan ahead while also leaving space to learn and iterate.

PLAN AHEAD

If you're not already planning your content, you need to—but not too much. Many influencers stress about having a tight enough plan. Or, when they don't have a plan, they make it a reason not to post. You don't need to have a finalized ready-to-execute content calendar at your disposal thirty or sixty days ahead. You only need to plan a week out and be aware of the content framework you are planning for the month. Especially if you are being really intentional about new growth. At that point, you have no idea what is going to work well. Planning past a week gives no room for learning and gathering data around what works. What happens if you plan thirty days of the shittiest content on earth? Cool. It's planned. Doesn't mean it will work. Staying within a week out is the most intelligent strategy because it lets you learn from the last week. If you see a post that got major engagement, post something similar the following week. You simply can't do that if you plan too far in advance.

Plan, post, track and learn, iterate, repeat. When I started doing Reels, people liked the ones where I talked about how to make money online. They didn't care about any other ones I did. I learned this because I got a lot of saves on those but not the others. So if a concept is working, do a lot more of it. You don't have to think, *I already posted one motivational piece this week so I should do something different.* Why? If it works, do more!

I've seen influencers put themselves in boxes because they think sticking with the same concept is too much. If it's getting the most engagement your audience is telling you what they like, so keep it up. Don't punish them by trying other things. It's not as sexy as we like to think it is sometimes. It's human nature to want to reinvent the wheel and be unique. We're creative beings. But sometimes the wheel works. Track, find out what works, and follow the trend.

When you get started, decide that you're going to test another vertical every other day. Or, do one vertical per week. Maybe you focus on motivation for one entire week. Then the next, it's all about education. The following week could then be about lifestyle. You decide what you're going to test, and your audience will tell you what they like or don't. Be strategic. Never post content simply because you like it. Or because someone else says it will work. Everyone's audience is different.

When you do plan, use a grid app like Later or Planoly. They allow you to drag and drop photos and rearrange them on the grid to see what the overall feed looks like if you posted these photos in that specific order. Ultimately, this will save you a lot of time and allow you to focus on day-to-day engagement with your current and ideal audience. It is also how you make sure your feed looks sick.

STREAMLINE YOUR FEED AESTHETIC

When your audience clicks your profile, their first view is

how your overall grid looks. Picking a style, theme, and aesthetic for that grid is critical to your success. You want to be remembered, not just noticed. So plan your feed aesthetic as part of your content plan. Consider the following:

- What are your brand definitions? (You did that already in Chapter 2.)
- What are your colors?
- What is your aesthetic inspiration? What accounts would you like to mirror?
- Build out a mood board so you can see your inspiration in action.

Once you've taken, sourced, and edited your content, the next step is to lay out your planned content before uploading so you can view the overall look and feel of your account and decide what post looks best in specific areas of the grid. The goal is to create a depth of field, similar to how you would in photography. Space out busy photos with a mix of more clean or minimal photos to achieve a nice balance.

Be mindful that these are all data-driven observations of Instagram audience behaviors. If you want to appeal to a large group of users, know that these are the creative rules that get the most engagement.

CREATE SAVABLE CONTENT

Savable content is another critical strategy you must deploy to grow and capture the attention of brands. If you visit "view insights," it'll tell you how many people saved your last post, which means they clicked the little badge to the far right of their screen to keep it. Saves are crucial due to the way Instagram's algorithm currently works. Instagram uses saves to determine how much engagement a post is getting. More saves equate to your post being shown to more people.

The most shared savable content is typically highly relevant, motivational, or educational. So share a tutorial, educate, motivate, and provide a means to solve a common issue within your audience. Always pick shareable topics that are relevant, relatable, and trending. People like to go back to inspiring images and quotes for motivation when they need it later.

You should be saving too. When I see great posts by other marketers I want to learn from, I save them. I save ads that I consider viral if they have over a million views to learn why they did so well. You can also save items that you are personally interested in to learn more about what you offer as an influencer. I save clothing. I save Reels. Create inspo collections and label them. Go back and see what you saved, and you might learn something new about yourself.

KEEP YOUR CAPTION GAME STRONG

Captions should be written like a conversation. And, in most cases, you should get to your point quickly. You only have about three seconds before a user decides to read your entire post or not. Always start with a powerful hook that piques the curiosity of your target demographic. Provide valuable tips within your niche, whether they be motivational, inspirational, personal stories, relatable humor or quotes, or product release alerts. Share your expertise, because your perceived post quality is so crucial to influencer growth.

Want to boost your engagement? Aim for longer captions that share a story or experience. You can write more and still get to the point in a reasonable amount of time. Long-form copy increases time spent on post. The point is to split copy lengths and see what your audience responds to the most.

Your platform is your place to share your personal experience, failure, mental health, loves and losses, and personal journey. Be authentic and share. If you're struggling, share it! Someone out there will appreciate what you did and you're going to help them in that moment. Loving a new brunch spot? Share it! Guarantee someone is looking for new food spots to check out. People crave connection naturally, so you're just giving people what they desire—connection. No one wants to feel alone. There is always someone who will resonate with what you're saying.

Give your audience a call to action within your post. What do you want them to do next? Follow you? Link in bio? Answer a question? Questions are always a compelling CTA for posts. Prompt your audience to engage in your comment section.

Use captions to foster community. Get your audience excited and make them feel like you create all posts or products specifically for them and fulfill their needs. Create community chains by introducing yourself and telling others to do the same "in the comments below." Then like-minded people and similar accounts can engage with each other on your post, and the algorithm will reward you.

Remember, one of the most profound human desires is to be understood. Write simple captions asking who can relate and watch as others repost, share, and comment. Don't be perfect. People crave authenticity on this platform. Any time you can be honest, do it. When you open up and are vulnerable with your audience, it makes you seem more relatable. You need users to be invested in your content to foster a genuine connection with your community. Instagram will see this engagement occurring on your account and promote you to like-minded people.

Since the algorithm favors engagement and time on the post, you want to force people to spend more than a few seconds with you. Get them to linger and explore. Take advantage of long-form copy to do so. Treat your feed like a micro blog, encouraging people to read what you have to say. Dive deep.

INSTAGRAM POST FREQUENCY

Frequency is an essential aspect of growth. Instagram gives priority to recent posts, which is why posting every day is to your advantage. You want your posts to show up as much as possible.

Instagram is a numbers game, so the more you post, the more you raise your chances of going viral and increasing your engagement.

Gary Vee recommends posting multiple times each day. I certainly agree with that from a brand perspective. But it comes down to how much time you have and how committed you are. Influencers always ask me how often to post. What works best is consistency more than a specific number. Post at least once a day, especially when you have a growth goal in mind.

Do not pull a Snoop Dog and post twenty times a day because you're never really giving enough time to optimize and learn.

More than mass volume, focus on producing and planning relevant content. Stories should be more frequent than posts, for sure. Posting your stories multiple times every single day is optimal because it's how you build solid relationships with your audience. The exact frequency depends on you.

Multiple stories a day engage with your audience and a minimum of one weekly post; three to five posts a week is an adequate standard if you choose not to post daily. Determine what works best for your audience as well. What are your best engagement days and hours? Do people care if you post every day? Make that determination and remember quality over quantity. Let your stories be your guaranteed daily engagement. Post when your audience is active. Check your analytics and use your data to determine the most engaged time for you.

TRACK YOUR METRICS!

Track your metrics so you know what content resonates and then post similar content. Follow the trends. Check your analytics reports every seven days and compare them to the previous seven days. Are you growing? Are you losing followers? If so, why? What about your engagement levels? When you see a topic is resonating, replicate it.

Don't get too crazy about it. Daily tracking might be a little bit much. It's like weighing yourself daily. Being overly focused on metrics might have you become hyperstressed, less creative, and unmotivated with the process. Nobody needs that stress. With Instagram, there is so much happening on the back end. They are constantly removing bots from people's accounts. You might lose followers in twenty-four hours but not in a bad way, and seeing it might freak you out. Focus on the grand trends. For instance, are you consistently up over thirty days? Are you consistently up over two weeks? That is more important than daily fluctuations.

Split test. Go back to your Heroes. Are they sharing a particular kind of style that maybe they don't often do that you see getting a lot of engagement? Even posts that aren't your Heroes but are getting a lot of engagement? Save them. Replicate what they are doing with your flavor. Change the copy to make it fit your audience. Maybe they have a great attention grabber. How can you use that attention grabber and make it fit your style?

AVOID CONTENT BLOCK

It happens to every creator out there, so it is bound to happen to you at some point if it hasn't already. Don't freak out. You can fight it. Follow what you've learned so far in this chapter. Plan ahead, map out your content verticals, and follow niche-related topics. You should never be stuck long in a content block.

One roadblock aversion is to save every post you come across that makes you think, *I love that!* Create a specific collection within Instagram for inspiration. Save the posts that have high engagement and also have an aesthetic you like. Go back to them to gather ideas when you're in the process of planning your content. Create inspiration boards on Pinterest and Tumblr of poses, lighting, color plays, outfits, presets and filters, and content topics.

Ultimately if you stay inspired, you will be inspiring.

TREAT SOCIAL MEDIA AS YOUR RÉSUMÉ

You wouldn't put a lousy headshot of yourself on a résumé, so stop using grainy-ass photos on Instagram. Make sure your content is clean, crisp, and clear.

Similarly, you wouldn't put categories or roles that are history and no longer make sense for the image you want to represent you on your résumé either. For instance, if I'm applying for a graphic design job, I'm not going to have McDonald's listed as a place I worked when I was sixteen. It is irrelevant.

Edit your platform if you decide that some of your earlier posts don't feel like you anymore or the image you want to present. Archive that shit if it was a pleasant memory in your life, or delete it altogether.

People are odd and have too much time. I have had people scroll and like pictures from 2016 when it's 2021. *Okay, you have scrolled, sir, for some time to go to this hideous photo of me. Why did you do that?* I just don't know sometimes.

Do your due diligence. Clean up your profile if you are not the same person. Make sure your image is what you want it to be. Show up strategically. This alone will drastically improve your engagement, but we'll cover more strategies for that in Chapter 5.

DO THIS NOW:

- What do you need to do to up your content game? Do you have a streamlined aesthetic and feed with great pictures and captions?
- Are your posts consistent?
- What is your engagement rate? Are you tracking it regularly? If not, you need to be. Build a spreadsheet today and do a weekly analysis.
- What are your macro, micro, and nano content verticals? Do some work to build them out. Use the Defining Your Content Verticals worksheet below as your guide.
- Are you planning your content one week in advance? What structure do you need to have in place to do this?
- Are you leveraging all the platforms you could be using? Are you on TikTok and YouTube?

CHAPTER 5

BOOST ENGAGEMENT

"If people see that you're passionate about what you're creating, they're going to enjoy it."

—DAVID DOBRIK

Building genuine connections with users is nonnegotiable if you want to grow an Instagram business. The algorithm will crush you if you don't. The key is to understand people better. Remember, the focus is connection over coin.

Your efforts should be to connect with your audience 80 percent of the time and provide value through your brand partnerships with the other 20 percent. If you're always focused on building good relationships with your community you will always be able to regularly monetize your account. Of course, you'll learn how to master all of this in the final chapters of this book. You can't market a bad Instagram account and expect success, which is why everything you have learned until now is so critical.

However, engagement does come in waves. The cycle of decline to decrease to increase is always happening due to the algorithm consistently testing and evolving. So do not beat yourself up if you notice a drop in followers when you're doing everything right. You will see a rise again.

Ultimately, brands will work with you based on these five criteria:

1. The relevance of your profile to their brand
2. Your engagement rate
3. Your follower count
4. The frequency of posts
5. Former experience and results

We've already talked about streamlining your brand, zeroing in on your niche and audience, and posting epic content. If you are doing all that, you can check off number one on that list (and likely three and four). Then, your focus will be to get people to spend time on your posts and feed. High-engagement posts get pushed to the top of people's feeds. Lower-engagement posts are pushed to the bottom.

ENGAGEMENT RATE BENCHMARKS

By now, you should understand that attention and influence are very different qualities. Ask yourself: do I only have my audience's attention, or do I have influence over what they do? Remember, brands who pay well on repeat want influencers who capture, hold, and grow influence, not just attention.

Your first job is to win the attention of your audience when they are scrolling through their feeds. How will you force them to stop, read, look, listen, watch, and engage? Your second job is to influence and inspire people to complete a particular action. If you're doing the first job well, you'll have a high engagement rate including for your CTAs.

Do you know what your engagement rate is? Brands don't want to work with someone who posts once a month, not because of the post frequency but because that would mean you don't have an engaged audience. You can't consider yourself an active community member of a group in real life if you only show up to the cookout once a year. That would be rather weird. Social media is no different.

Brands value influencers who post meaningful captions as well, so don't just post two or three emojis all the time. Hearting comments does not encourage genuine engagement. It would be super shitty to have a million followers and little engagement because you never found your tribe of people who related to you and loved and learned from you. Comments and saves matter more than anything, so building a highly engaged community within a specific niche is critical to the success of your Instagram career. Relevant content and authenticity are the key factors in achieving this quickly.

Suppose you do not have experience or results in doing brand partnerships. That is not a deal breaker. Companies care about actionable data when working with influencers the right way. Not fluff metrics. So, where do you stand? Here are the benchmarks for industry-standard engagement rates:

- Under 10k followers: 2–10 percent
- 10k–100k followers: 1–5 percent
- 100k followers and up: 1–5 percent

Most influencers have attention and maybe trust, but few have true influence. Being likable and trustworthy isn't hard. How many people do *you* follow that you like and trust as a human but do not give 100 percent authority to suggest a product, brand, service, or experience? If you're like most people, that number is probably tiny—maybe 1 percent.

If you are not a credible resource who falls in people's 1 percent, it's because you have not revealed yourself to be so. You have to graduate to the next step—build credibility, which only happens through shared experience, your ability to prove results, and your ability to speak to what you stand for.

When an influencer has a high engagement rate it shows a brand their followers are paying attention. The likelihood of them taking action when an influencer posts about a product or service becomes higher too. Generally, you want your engagement rate to be around 2–3 percent while 4–6 percent is excellent. Any number above that and you are doing far better than most. But, remember, the influencer industry is always changing, so always stay plugged into industry benchmarks.

I have worked with dozens of brands with mega, macro, and micro influencers who couldn't move products for shit because their audiences don't believe their recommendations are valuable to their lives. Honestly, I'm tired of seeing surface-level shit on the platform. It's one reason why I wrote this book. Brands want to work with the titans of influence in their space. So, let's get you there.

TWO PRACTICES TO SKYROCKET YOUR ENGAGEMENT

If you have at least one thousand followers and a proper niche, you can get a brand to pay you. And remember, being hot is not a niche. Think bigger. To consistently drive engagement, there are two critical engagement practices to do constantly:

1. Prospecting engagement
2. Retention engagement

Strategically engage more and your engagement will rise. The key to this is to show up to the platform with intention. Treat social media like real life. How would you communicate with actual people? Start conversations. Leave users questions and compliments and comments that encourage a response. And above all, offer value by giving people what they want and need.

I hate to bring it up again but clean your list if you haven't done this already. Make this a regular practice. Fake followers—the ghosts who follow you—will hurt you way more than they help because they don't engage. I know it sucks to see your follower count drop fast, but if you are cleansing your list of the inactive spammers, you might have a smaller community but a higher engagement rate.

For a micro influencer, your number of fake followers should not be higher than 15 percent. Anything above that should be considered a cause for concern. And again, do not buy into fast success tactics—they will only hurt you. Fame audit yourself regularly to see what brands see when their social media representatives look you up. Google yourself and pretend you are thinking about hiring you. Would you? Then commit to fostering genuine engagement through prospecting engagement and retention engagement.

PROSPECTING ENGAGEMENT

Prospecting engagement is the practice of engaging with like-minded accounts that do not yet follow and engage with you. You must engage with prospecting audiences one to two hours a day minimum if you want to grow.

When prospecting, do not do the follow/unfollow/repeat old-ass strategy. Most people will know what I'm talking about here. Don't follow someone and like six posts to get them to follow you and then unfollow them. It's kind of creepy and so Bumble. (Could you at least buy me a drink first?) Just because a person likes your stuff doesn't mean you should follow them back. Pass! It's also not a good strategy because there's no engagement involved. If you just like posts to get people to follow you, that is not fostering a community. It doesn't work. People will catch on to you and think you're a weirdo.

Gary Vee's $1.80 strategy is solid. Every day you put your two cents—meaning research and comment—on nine posts for ten different hashtags that are relevant to your niche. If you add that up it equates to $1.80, which is why he calls it that.

Comment on your Hero 25, 50, and 100's posts. Engage with

top commenters on the posts, and then go to their profiles and engage with them in their personal stories and most recent posts. Make yourself noticed and appreciated. It's brilliant... and time-consuming. But all great things cost time. So, invest that time because people will see that. People often try to make it something that it's not, but the platform is about relationships. Don't get caught up with follower count and become robotic and distracted from the community.

The idea is to have and build real connections with human beings. It's like complimenting someone on the sidewalk. I might remember your face for five seconds, but I'm going to forget the next day. I don't know your name. I don't know anything about you. We didn't have a conversation. Maybe I liked your hat, but that's it. The same experience happens when you leave an emoji on someone's post. It's a nice gesture, but there is no depth to it. Be memorable.

Implement the same strategy with your top ten hashtags. Here is how to do that:

1. Search the hashtag
2. View the above-the-fold posts—the top nine posts in Top, Recent, and Reels for the hashtag
3. Leave a thoughtful comment (your two cents) on those nine posts and engage with the top commenters

It's a constructive process to get in front of more engaged eyes. Turn on the post notifications for your Hero 25, and at the very least, leave a comment on their post as quickly as humanly possible, so they will see and respond to your comment. Then, after you've left a comment, go back within the hour of the post going live and respond to at least three or four comments with a thoughtful and intriguing response that organically encourages them to respond to you, click your profile, and follow.

Do this at least four times a week, if not every day if you can, for ninety days. Then the next ninety days, move on to your next twenty-five Heroes. The most engaged audience on your Hero 100 is always looking through the comments. You want and need their eyes on your profile. So you need to show up and engage on these posts.

Get into it. Be genuine. Pretend it's a conversation in real life. To take it a step further, DM a compliment via audio message or video that will leave a lasting impression. Audio messages are great because they pique people's interests, where a photo can sometimes feel too random.

I've had a few instances where people sent me audio messages and we built solid connections from there. So many people have a story where they have established a great relationship with someone they met through social media.

I once posted a screenshot of one of my favorite books, *Connected to Goodness* by David Meltzer, the former sports super-agent and CEO of Leigh Steinberg Sports & Entertainment agency, the inspiration of Tom Cruise's titular character in *Jerry Maguire*, and TV host of the shows *Office Hours* and *2 Minute Drill*. I have read it about four times and often have it in my ears as the audiobook I take on walks. A guy who was following me sent me a message because he knew the author. Meltzer had mentored him. He was also in the influencer space. We had a lot in common and swapped a few emails. Eventually, I interviewed him for my Micro Influencer Academy because he is a manager for influencers. Connections like this are truly amazing and one reason I love social media. It's great to meet new Insta friends and even better when they become longtime connections.

RETENTION ENGAGEMENT

Retention is the practice of engaging with your current audience so you can keep them. To maintain your following, engage with preexisting audiences one hour per day minimum.

The first thirty minutes to an hour of posting is critical for your post's success and defines whether or not that post has the opportunity to go semiviral and end up on the Explore page. Engage with everyone who leaves comments so that Instagram sees that your post is getting a lot of traction. The algorithm might even put it on the Explore page and give it an additional push. The first hour is crucial, because you want to help Instagram see that your post is good.

I did this as a split test on myself. I purposely did not engage and let people comment. Then I did it the other way. I posted and engaged with someone, and more people commented because they thought I would respond to them too, which I did.

When you think about it, it's weird *not* to respond to someone who left something nice on your posts. It's rude. Someone is complimenting you. And you're like not saying anything back? You likely would not behave that way in real life. Give yourself a thirty-to-forty-five-minute window of time to respond before you get focused on work or something else. Join the comments on your posts for retention. Don't leave emojis only. Leave comments that resonate with the audience. Make it something that will make people stop and read and leave a response.

Now, let me give you an easy win: *don't* like the comments on your post until you have new content to post so that you can go like all the comments on your previous post immediately after you upload something new. Those who interacted in your comment section will be notified that you engaged with them and will most likely go check out your new post.

Another important note is to focus on how much reach your posts are getting, more than your focus on likes. Reach is the total number of people who have seen your content. Impressions are the number of times a person has seen your content. Creating shareable content expands your reach. Graphic posts lead to more shares and reach due to Instagram's ranking system. Remember that time spent on a post is graded in the Instagram algorithm as high value.

Easily increase time spent on your posts by implementing long-form copy, story-based copy, or getting people to swipe through a carousel of photos. High-engagement posts that we typically see get the most engagement for micro, nano, and macro influencers always have their faces in them or are text-based graphic posts. Questions also do well. These are consistent strategies for real brand growth. Ask questions every ten days if once a week is too much. And share when people send questions. Answer them publically when appropriate. Great questions are straightforward:

- What do you guys want to learn more about?
- What would you be interested in seeing in my account more?
- What are your greatest challenges?

People will respond because everyone has an opinion. Whenever you post questions, I guarantee you will get at least one response.

Stories are by far the most effective daily means of retention. Start valuing your views and understand that consistency is the key to story success. You have to be consistent with your story game as a way to create deep day-to-day engagement with your core audience. Start to think of your bare minimum story schedule like your typical food schedule. You most likely eat in the morning, afternoon, and night.

Take advantage of all of the engagement tactics available in IG stories like polls and quizzes. Ask your community to ask you questions. You might do a weekly twenty-five dollar Starbucks giveaway. People love gift cards or a free product for one lucky follower. Your engagement possibilities are endless. Get people engaged with your content to stay longer on the platform and interact later with ads and Instagram will reward you.

Remember to always add your post to your story as well. After you post, let people know you have a new post up. You are likely to have a way higher engagement rate in your views and interactions with your stories than posts, so use that to your advantage.

CRICKETS ARE CLUES

If no one responds to you, that's not bad. You are learning that no one is engaged. Cool. But, why? Get curious. Here are some questions to ask:

- Do I need to rebrand?
- Do I need to connect with more people in my target demographic (do more prospecting engagement, perhaps)?
- Are my posts boring, confusing, or not grabbing attention?

One of those variables isn't on track, that's all. So experiment. Play with posts and make changes. Try again. Engagement is challenging, and often why people join Built to Influence. We are always finding and sharing new strategies for engagement. So, stick with it. Once you crack the code to find out what resonates, it becomes easier.

Join the Built to Influence community at built2influence. com to learn the most effective engagement strategies to skyrocket your brand and grow your following.

Maintain a positive mindset. Be clear on your *why*, be patient, and remember success doesn't usually happen overnight. You are building an influencer business. It is a process. Consider it like a career you are starting. Learning strategies doesn't automatically make you an expert. At this stage, you might be a junior media buyer, not the CEO. You will have some wins and failures, but it will all amount to your success if you're smart and stay optimistic. As an influencer, always remember:

Consistency is key. Content is king. Engagement is *coin*.

Your focus must always be on increasing your growth, reach, and engagement. Your goal is to impress brands and give them an irresistible opportunity. Make them believe they need to work with you because it will greatly benefit their brand.

DO THIS NOW:

- Analyze your engagement rate. Where do you stand in relation to the benchmarks? Create an engagement rate goal and then consider what you need to do to get there.
- Make sure prospecting engagement and retention engagement are two strategies you are focused on. How do you ensure you are spending one hour focused on each practice per day?
- What posts have you done that are most successful, with the highest engagement? Do more! Do less of the posts that got the least engagement.

CHAPTER 6

REACH-OUTS

"I work harder than every single person I know, and the only person that is on the same level as me is my brother. If you look at the top social media stars, it's me and him. I think that's our advantage. We're not the prettiest; we're not even the funniest, we're not the wittiest, whatever it is."

—JAKE PAUL

The thought of saying "I have an agent" might make you feel like a baller, but no one pitches you better than *you*. Plus, unless you have millions of followers, no agent will go to bat for you like they would for someone they know they can make more money from. You might think you need one because they know how to negotiate better than you or understand contracts. Or because you have a bazillion tasks to focus on. But you are the best one for the job.

So many influencers hire agents thinking they can help them maximize and capitalize off their talent, but instead, they end up doing 75 percent of the work while the agent lines up some subpar deals.

It happened to one influencer, Gigi Robinson @itsgigirobinson, who I spoke to during the creation of this book. She told me about a time when she hired an agent she thought she needed, and felt she could trust, who let her down. She was not a makeup influencer, but her agent pitched her as one because he thought she had a look. "It was heartbreaking for me, and I'm not alone dealing with this...a ton of influencers deal with agents taking advantage and not having their talents' best interest," Gigi told me.

In this chapter, you will learn everything you need to know about how to pitch yourself. You will learn how to show (rather than tell) your worth and present yourself so brands can see you are serious. And you'll be prepared long before a deal is offered to you because you'll stand out. To do all this, you need a slick media kit, a rate sheet, case studies, and to look like a damn professional.

Typically brands are looking at multiple influencers at a time, and depending on their allotted influencer budget, they will work with a few to split test their results with each. How they pick these lucky few has to do with their internal ranking system. They rank opportunities with each influencer based on their audience worth, engagement rate, aesthetic, pricing, and previous results. The goal is to wow them every single freaking time.

You will negotiate with a brand's marketing department or executive team, so you need to look damn good—like you are prepared and know how to execute a job well done. Please don't wait to create your portfolio until they ask you for it. Be prepared to send it immediately. A lot of deals are very time-sensitive.

You will likely have to send out hundreds of pitches for reach-outs but will only land a handful. If that bothers you, get out of this game. You will be disappointed. Anyone who pitches themselves for a living knows you cannot take it personally.

If you fail, keep going. Your job is to pitch so much that when you win, you think, *Oh, that's cool*, but it doesn't make or break you. Getting a lot of nos from pitches is what you signed up for. If you don't do that, then you're not going to win. A lot of nos is a great indicator you might need to work on your content quality, honing your niche, and engagement rate. If you're constantly being rejected, there is likely a very clear reason why. Don't ignore it. Learn from it.

And if you think that brand deals are going to come to you, the reality is there are millions of influencers. You have got to put yourself out there to be seen as an authority figure. It's why I asked you up front why you want to be an influencer. Never lose sight of your reason. Take every action through that lens, especially when pitching yourself and making money as an influencer.

Now, there are three ways to do that, so let's get into them.

THE THREE AVENUES FOR REVENUE

Unlike most people, you don't have to build the next innovative widget to sell or compel everyone to buy your service. You have the potential for at least three streams of income relatively quickly. They are:

1. Sponsored posts
2. Affiliate marketing opportunities
3. Selling your own products or services

SPONSORED POSTS

These are opportunities where you offer brands to promote their product or service for a specific rate not dependent upon results. They can be posts, stories, highlight placement, or content marketing spots on your other social channels. Sponsored posts are the type of deal influencers make the most money from, so it should be your focus to land paid sponsorship as often as possible.

AFFILIATE MARKETING

A brand affiliate program is when you promote a brand's products or services and earn a commission on every purchase your audience makes. There are thousands of affiliate platforms out there. Do some research relevant to your niche and find as many high-paying opportunities out there as you can. Some of the most popular affiliates are with Airbnb, Booking.com, Commission Junction, and ShareASale. Many large corporations have programs where you can immediately sign up directly on their platform to earn a commission payment for every sale you drive from your profile.

On this, please know that many affiliate marketing companies or programs will say, *Be our ambassador and we'll give you 10 percent off...*or send you free stuff, or you can buy stuff and then promote it for free. True brand ambassadorships are where you're sought out or selected through an application process. Brands like Chipotle, Best Buy, and Lululemon offer social media challenges or competitions where applicants submit, go through a bidding process, and are chosen and adequately compensated both with product and payment.

SELL YOUR OWN PRODUCTS AND SERVICES

We live in such an entrepreneurial society. Almost everybody has a Shopify store and sells their products or tries at some point. With some investment on your part, you can sell your own collection of niche-relevant products and make a killing too. I see people doing this first then deciding to be an influencer. Popular products to sell include:

- E-books
- Photography products
- Videos
- Digital art and graphics
- Audio files
- Physical products on e-commerce sites

Selling your own products is powerful because you're not relying on anyone else to deliver. You don't need to do this, but it might be an avenue you consider once you have established a community.

Similar ways to monetize are available to all influencers who use YouTube. But there are some slight differences on that platform, so let's also go over those.

YOUTUBE MONETIZATION STRATEGIES

YouTube is one of the most established platforms for influencers and a space you want to be on and monetize if you are serious about growth. As with any social platform, having a clearly defined niche will help you earn more. There are many ways to monetize your YouTube channel:

Use Affiliate Links to Earn Commission

You can request affiliate opportunities from the brands you choose to promote on top of your fee for posting if you believe it will have a high sales volume. Popular affiliate sponsorships for YouTube include:

- Amazon
- Skillshare
- Target
- Pointsprizes
- Movavi

Commissions range from 5–15 percent.

Become a YouTube Partner and Earn from Video Ads

For many YouTubers, advertising revenue is a significant portion of their monthly earnings. To become a partner and earn the ability to set up Adsense, you need one thousand followers and four thousand video watch hours in the past twelve months to apply. Your account must also follow their rules for monetization to avoid any copyright issues. Those rules are:

- Posting content that is deemed inappropriate or stolen cannot be monetized.
- If you use another creator's content you must add value to any third-party content. Share original commentary, educational value, or editorialized statement.
- Make sure your channel follows YouTube policies and guidelines, and there aren't any active community guidelines strikes against your account.
- Make sure that two-step verification is turned on for your Google account.

Once you apply, your channel will be reviewed by an actual human, so it can take up to a year to be approved. Some marketing experts say if you do not receive a response within a month, you most likely will not be approved. If you get rejected, apply again in thirty days, but ensure that you review all content before reapplying to ensure you have not violated the rules. Click Monetization in the navigation menu, then YouTube will automatically track your progress. Once you are eligible, you can click Apply Now.

YouTube partners can turn on ads, channel membership, a merchandise shelf, super chat, stickers, and premium revenue. Anytime someone watches your video and then pays for premium, you earn a part of what they pay for premium. You can also sign up for Patreon or similar community platforms where your fans pay to access exclusive content and live discussions, or tip you for a job well done.

Of course, you can also sell your own products through YouTube. Sellfy is recommended because it's designed for YouTubers.

For YouTube there are two types of branded partnership deals:

Branded content. Content paid for by a brand that featured its products or services.

Brand deals. This is also called brand sponsorship. It is a partnership between creators.

Brand integrations. When a creator finds a seamless way to feature a brand or product review, typically along with other brands, this is known as a brand integration. To find brands for integrations, use YouTube Brand Connect.

Ultimately, the key to landing paid brand deals and monetizing is by displaying your worth. Alex Stewart of @ aftertheisland worked as a beauty publicist for four years before she launched and that taught her what stood out in a pitch. She said there is a difference between impersonal and overused pitches versus ones that are unique and authentic. We will talk about that soon. But, before any reach-out happens, take her advice to heart. "When I pitch myself I am always enthusiastic about the brand and do a ton of research to make sure I love the product and my beliefs match with theirs," she said.

Her number one rule is to never work with a brand she doesn't 100 percent believe in. Maintaining your transparency and authenticity with your audience should be your top priority as an influencer.

YouTuber Sonya Esman @sonyaesman would probably agree. She said she gets brand partnerships mostly through experience, reputation, and the trust that she's acquired throughout the years. Many influencers, like Esman, build through personal referrals. So, show up, post great content, interact, and have an impressive portfolio. And that is how you make $4,000–$10,000 per month like these YouTubers and so many others.

BUILD AN IMPRESSIVE PORTFOLIO LIKE THE PROS

You are officially a self-marketer now, so you need to have a portfolio that presents an enticing image for brands. With all the platforms and tools available today, it's not hard to make a portfolio that looks great. From a design standpoint, there are platforms like Canva that make everyone a professional designer. There are so many great templates there that designers upload themselves. Visit Canva and search "Influencer Media Kit" to get hundreds of templates. All you have to do is find one that fits your aesthetic. Drag, drop, done.

Always use the best photo (headshot) you have of yourself, and a bio that clearly and concisely defines your niche, passions, and what you bring to the table for any brand. And showcase your social stats like:

- Followers per platform
- Engagement rates
- Reach

- Impressions
- Viewership
- Audience demographics

YouTube analytics to showcase are:

- Growth forecast
- Audience retention and engagement
- Influential users in your audience
- The ratio of male to female followers

As an influencer, your product is your audience. The metrics to showcase are your follower count per platform, engagement rates, reach and impressions, viewership, and audience demographics. Don't go super crazy with showcasing your creative vision at this point. Less is more. Be prepared to share your previous brand work you've done, and add those logos, brand testimonials, and sponsored content photography you have. Of course, also include your contact information.

If you need more support, we detail creating a yes-worthy influencer portfolio in our Micro Influencer Academy and have a private Facebook group that trains you on how to land the best deals. Join us at built2influence.com.

Create variations of your media kit for each vertical as you pitch more brands and get more partnerships. If you're pitching a fitness brand, you should only have fitness-related photos in that portfolio. Always include brands you've worked with when they are competitors. When a brand sees that you have worked with other brands, they might be more likely to want to work with you. Brand testimonials are also important. You might not be here yet and that's okay. You can get there pretty easily. If you're not at the stage, this is where taking TFP (trade for post) partnerships with larger brands is great. You want to be able to show you have reputable experience in the industry, so if you can slap a logo on your portfolio from Dyson, L'Oreal, or Target because they gifted you a product to promote, it's a serious win. It will help your ability to land paid deals in the near future. Ask for a written testimonial from the brand representative you worked with during that deal. Quote the positive things they said about you in your portfolio.

Brands see thousands of portfolios and a lot of bad ones. You set yourself apart when you look like a professional. They get a mixed bag, from the people who think, *I don't deserve anything*, to the Beyoncés who believe everyone should want to work with them. (Somebody come up with a reality TV show on that, 'cause I would watch that all day.) When you show up with a conversion-worthy portfolio, you immediately get past the first selection criteria.

HOW BRANDS VET AND SELECT INFLUENCERS

Every brand has an internal ranking system for how they select influencers. The questions they ask tend to be:

1. Do we like this person's aesthetic?
2. What is their number of followers?
3. What are their engagement rates?

When they are vetting, you either fall off or stay in the pile as they go down the pack. Let's say Mallory and Jay are in the same running. The marketing team might consider who has worked with more brands. If Jay's a little higher now, maybe Mallory's not out, but Jay might beat her because he has experience. But that's not all. They also factor in price. Mallory is $500 cheaper, and she has a slightly higher engagement rate than Jay. So, she might win. It's a balancing act. Maybe they say yes to both. There's no specific method to the madness, but teams are generally considering the same criteria.

Over time, the nos won't be as bad as they might be in the beginning, but expect a lot of them. You are not going to land every client you want. I don't. No one does. But you will have a higher success rate than most because you are using all these strategies combined. I have a high close and retention rate. Why? Because I learn from my experiences and take time to understand my potential clients' actual desires, not their presented ones.

Always keep your engagement high. Doing too many sponsored content posts can make your engagement suffer, and we'll talk more about this in the next chapter. Let's say you have a hundred thousand followers and an 8 percent engagement rate. That means you could roughly negotiate $8,000 a post without even factoring exclusivity, usage, and deliverability timeline. How would you like that four times a month? I've seen it done many times.

JOIN INFLUENCER MARKETING PLATFORMS

After your portfolio is complete, get on every legitimate influencer marketing platform. They are constantly changing. At

Built to Influence, we share the best current list of influencer platforms for micro influencers.

Brands go to these platforms and post opportunities. There are trade opportunities, which means you get a free product for posting, and they'll give you the post and qualifications they want.

There are also compensation opportunities that are used as influencer bait where an influencer pitches themselves and their quote for the project.

A brand might also offer a rate like $600 for a particular project. On those projects, there's minimal room for negotiation, but still always try. They might also post affiliate opportunities for you to get paid as an ambassador and get a percentage on what you sell. Each deal varies, but the benefit of affiliate opportunities is that they force you to know your audience, sit with yourself, and know what the demographic that actively engages with you is into. Once you're clear on your audience you will know which affiliate deal is really good for you and you'll feel confident pushing sales because it is a no-brainer offer to your audience.

There are all kinds of platforms to check if you have a channel to push sales through. Aspire HQ is a big one. There is also Grin. Octoly is another trade-only platform for the industry's biggest brands.

Brands pay upwards of $40,000 a year to be on these platforms because they have faith in this kind of influencer marketing. So especially when you start, take big gigs with brands even if you don't get paid much but can use your affiliation with them to continue to build. Don't knock the unpaid sponsorship opportunities for brands you believe in, brands that you would buy from, and those that would integrate well with your brand and ultimately be appreciated by your audience.

You can use those deals to help you snag higher-paid brand partnerships in the future. Who cares that the value of the perfume is a hundred dollars, and you have a thousand followers, and you make zero dollars for a one-time post? If it's coming from one of the legendary well-known brands, its logo will look good on your portfolio. It's a signal to other brands you're the real deal. It changes the conversation when you go to a brand to be paid.

There are a lot of big brands on these platforms, so it's a good idea to do reach-outs and pitch yourself there at least once a month.

HOW TO FIND BRAND CONTACTS

Long gone are the days when finding brand contacts takes forever. It's unnecessary to spend hours searching online for the people you want to contact. There are dozens of extensions you can download to your browser that will scrape and extract email addresses for any website.

Hunter IO is one I like to use, although there are many. You want to find real people when using these scraper tools, not "hello@" or "info@" addresses. Look for a name, like tony@adidas.com (totally made up; don't get excited). You can also find almost any brand contact via LinkedIn.

Simply enter the brand name in the search bar and scroll through to "people." These are individuals who work for the company and their roles are always listed.

Also search for specific keywords for roles that have the power. Avoid speaking to the social media intern. Go to the social media director, PR manager, or influencer marketing director. These are the people who will give you the red or green light.

In Built to Influence, we try to make it as easy as possible for our students so we offer them access to our brand database, which is filled with over five thousand brands' contacts and is organized by vertical and contact.

HOW TO PITCH

When pitching, reference the value you bring and your awareness of the brand and what they stand for. Prove it's not a generic reach-out. You might mention, *I saw you had a partnership with @xinfluencer, and that your products are a, b, and c, and my audience is all about supporting brands who value this. Can you connect me with the person who handles influencer partnerships for your company?* Show that you indeed have taken a few moments from your life to do your brand research. Hell, even quote some of their posts or site banner headlines and say why they resonate with you. Just be a human. It works. So get the email. The point is to contact the person with the power to pay you.

Use sentence cases in your emails and messages. It looks way more personal. Sentence case looks like this, with no caps on every letter. Not Like This, Because That's A Style Used in Marketing.

Keep your outreach concise. The point is to get a social media representative to ask so you can share more. Pique curiosity, then dive deep. Do not overshare. Treat first contact like a first date in real life. Don't give all skillsets away in the initial outreach. Don't seem desperate by playing hard to get. Keep it cool, like you want to work with them but not too badly, so you maintain the power.

Here is a reach out template you can use once you have the email address of the person you can negotiate with:

Hi <FIRST NAME>,

It's great to e-meet you! I wanted to know if you have any upcoming influencer partnerships available as I am a huge fan of BRAND NAME.

I love <PRODUCT NAME BECAUSE #1 AND #2> and would be thrilled to share it with my followers.

You can find me @YOUR INSTAGRAM HANDLE and on Facebook at <URL>.

I want to create:

<THREE TO FIVE BULLET POINTS ON THE SPECIFIC CONTENT STRATEGY YOU HAVE IN MIND FOR THIS PARTNERSHIP>.

Let me know if this interests you.

(Optional, no stress if this is your first one:) I have previously worked with <RELATED VERTICAL—BRAND NAME> and <BRAND NAME>, and we were able to achieve great things together. I hope we will too!

Looking forward to hearing from you,

<YOUR NAME>

We have dozens of brand reach-out templates for almost every scenario you will face as an influencer in our Built to Influence Academy. Join our community at built2influence. com for the most up-to-date information on advancing your influencer career.

Also, facts are always helpful. They show you know what you're talking about. They are always changing too, so google before you share. Here are three examples of the type of stats that are best:

- Eighty-four percent of millennials don't trust traditional advertising
- Seventy-four percent of customers identify word of mouth as a key influencer in their purchasing decision
- Eighty-eight percent of people trust online reviews written by other consumers as much as they trust recommendations from personal contacts

SELL STUFF YOU LOVE

Since you care about the community you've built and the

future one you're building, you will be mindful of what products and brands you are willing to recommend to your audience. No matter the glamor or the money being presented to you, if the product is shit, do not promote it. If it goes against your values, don't promote it.

Influencers who value their audience more than the quick buck are the ones brands want to work with and will pay very well. An influencer who maintains trust with their audience is an influencer that a brand can trust to promote their products. Be that type of influencer.

It's a people game before it's a profit game. Master that mindset. Any influencer who constantly throws branded content down their audience's throat will discover it messes up engagement. I've seen too many big influencers do it. There might be money to be made, but some people can get greedy with humans who won't stick around long. People don't want to see heavily branded content. It's not why you or anyone else signed up for the platform. It also gets confusing if you are promoting donuts one day and hair serum the next. So, be consistent.

When influencers promote products that don't make sense for their niche or push products too often, it's a turnoff. If you overdo it, you might have a fantastic year, but the next year will be super shitty because brands don't like that. Your audience doesn't like that either. Your engagement rate will go down.

POLL YOUR AUDIENCE

One solid tactic is to poll your audience on future designs and prototype products for the brand and your audience's feedback, comments, opinions on colors, usage, and materials. It is invaluable knowledge for a marketing team that could ultimately save a company tens of thousands, if not more.

I once polled my audience at a workshop I wanted to host outside the country. We had about 1,500 people respond, which was incredible because I asked a lot of questions. So, ask, ask, ask! *What do you look for in a good shoe?* That's a prime example of a great question. Most people would answer just because everyone likes shoes and everyone's got an opinion and wants to express it. People like questions that make them think a little bit.

Once the product goes to launch, ask for a kickback specifically on that product's sales. You already know your audience is interested, you know you'll make money, and you've already invested in it like they are. You could quickly request a 20-30 percent affiliate commission on any product you push on top of your posting fee after this testing period is done.

Brands need your recommendation to further social impact. Don't be afraid to charge your worth. Charge what the market will pay, not what you think you are worth, and raise your prices as you gain more experience. Quality social proof is one of the most coveted achievements a brand can achieve. So, charge, my friend, charge. Because if you recommend a product to your audience, and they recommend it to their friends, you've then created a beautiful continuum of conversion-worthy buzz.

You do need to eat (and enjoy a luxurious life), and you can't constantly throw promotions at your audience, so charge more for less. Work to build an engaged audience that is so in tune with who you are that you only need three or four partnerships a month to pay your bills and then some. If you rarely promote, your audience will notice when you do and believe that the products you promote must be worth their attention and money. Brands cannot survive without credibility. Leverage that because, if you're doing it right, you have exactly what they need.

Get brands to grow with you and grow your audience. Most companies will continually invest if it's good exposure for them. Audiences value and notice repetitive brand partnerships because it becomes believable that the influencer values the brand on a level that surpasses monetary gain, which it should. If it doesn't, your audience will read right through to that reality. Remember, the goal of a brand, specifically its marketing director, is to maximize a budget. As a person who has served as one to a few brands over the years, trust me—this is always top of mind. It's not about the number of eyes an influencer can provide. It's about the strength and resonating power their words hold within their audience.

AVOID SCAMMERS

Unfortunately, there are many influencer scams out there that target content creators. There are many best practices you can follow to ensure you never fall into one.

Do your research. First and foremost, don't look dumb. Check the sender's email account domain first to see if it's redirecting to the company's main website. Often, brands have different outreach email domains so they don't bog down their main domain. Do not be alarmed, but be smart and reach out via DM if you're a tad suspicious that their outreach doesn't come from a branded email.

If you receive a message with numerous grammatical errors, or they don't address you by name or username, or the URLs included appear suspicious, it might be a spammer. If you are asked for your Instagram password or asked to pay for delivery for a free item, it's smart to pass. You don't have time for nefarious activities like this. Follow your gut. If an opportunity appears to be too good to be true, it might be. It's not always the case. Don't default to assumptions of fraud. You will not look wise when you reach out to the brand's Instagram. Kindly ask if this is their email. You are not the fraud police, so don't go at anyone with your statements of certainty of fraud. *Kindly* ask. If it seems fishy, take ten minutes to study the brand before responding or clicking a link.

If someone is asking for your banking information, that's a hard no. Suppose the company does not have a representative who will sign a contract—also a no. Do your research. Never assume.

MAINTAINING TENACITY

I have found you have to be tenacious to be a successful entrepreneur. You're a micro influencer, and you work for yourself now. If you do not have that level of tenacity to keep doing it, believing that you're great and continuing to get better, you will not succeed. You have to constantly work on your content game, increase your engagement, and meet new people.

A micro influencer on our newsletter reached out to me one day because she felt hopeless. She told me she'd sent out pitches but hadn't heard anything back. When I asked her how many brands she reached out to, she told me five. Five is nothing. She needed to pitch way more. That is life as an influencer. Very rarely do brands immediately reach back out.

Brands are not your mommy. They don't think you're the best thing ever without you effectively displaying why you are. It's business. Entrepreneurship is challenging. No one is there to tell you you're great immediately. If you don't have that urgency and the drive to keep following up, it's not going to work.

A brand might want to work with you but aren't getting back right away because they are busy running multimillion- or billion-dollar companies. It's not you. It's them. You are a blip in the universe of what they need to get done. So you have to stay on top of reaching out and following up. Be persistent.

I have experienced this personally. When I get overwhelmed, it's because I lack clarity. Getting back to the goals you are working towards and determining your next step are so important. I was fortunate to learn from a mentor early on when I was starting: if you lack clarity on anything—about a relationship or business—you have nothing. You will always feel overwhelmed and never reach your goals. "You can do anything," he used to say. "The only ceiling you have is between you and God, and that comes down to your clarity. So get clear and bring yourself back when you need to."

Most people are hardworking. I think the people who will read this book are super hardworking, but you can't outwork a shitty plan or lack thereof. So you have to have clarity. And it's so funny—when I have clarity, I don't seem to work as hard, but I get better results. And I'm less stressed because I understand the course I'm on.

You also need to strategize and plan ahead. Write that shit out. Be intentional. Develop a budget for yourself. This is your career. You need a nice camera. You might need to budget for new outfits every month. Plan blocks of time that you can move around. Maybe you take a walk to get centered. Do what you need to do to be clear. If you're not, you might feel hopeless, feel stressed, or lack the tenacity to keep going.

I go for walks. I throw on music, or I walk in silence (yeah, like a creeper). I let my brain speak to me. The world starts to make sense when it's quiet. I get quiet and think about what's in my heart and mind. Clarity produces confidence. And not a false sense of it where you need to tell yourself you're the best, but becoming settled in what you're up to.

Either followers and brands love you, or they don't. There are other clients. There are billions of brands. Be less attached to a specific outcome and more attached to the clarity of where you want your life to go.

And stick to your guns. Companies need you. According to eMarketer.com, 75 percent of marketers say that finding the right influencers is the hardest part of influencer marketing. You will solve that issue for them. You will make it easy for them to choose you by presenting your data and passion, and then showing them why you are the right pick. Master the strategies of the next chapter, and you'll never sell a day in your life.

DO THIS NOW:

- Consider if there is more you could be doing to monetize. If there is, put a strategy together.
- Build an impressive portfolio. Don't wait until you have a deal. Be prepared.
- Start pitching yourself. (More about that in the next chapter too.)
- Are you on influencer marketing platforms? Get on immediately. There are many opportunities waiting for you from big brands.
- Remember if anything ever looks spammy, avoid it. Stay safe.

CHAPTER 7

BRAND DEALS & NEGOTIATIONS

"I believe in karma, and I believe if you put out positive vibes to everybody, that's all you're going to get back."

—KESHA

"Man, I wish brands would pay me more." I hear this far too often from micro influencers starting out when they price.

The negotiators on the brand side are always going to talk you down. Have no fear of pitching a more considerable sum because then you have room to negotiate. Always offer more value too. Don't simply settle or take what you can get. Often the work involved is more than what you're providing with that mindset.

Imagine a company paying you one hundred dollars for one post and one story that you think will take you one hour, but it takes you three because you pose and realize maybe you're not Gigi Hadid. In the end you have to take a hundred shots, travel to a specific location, and buy two props. By the time you finish, if you've spent more than two hours, it's probably not worth it. You could spend that at Starbucks in a week.

Think carefully about your time. Do the math. What you're doing might be enjoyable but separate the work aspect from the pleasure. Be a wise businessperson. You are not just someone who has cute photos and videos. You are a professional. You understand how the platform works and why you're valuable there.

Let's use the iPhone as a quick example. The iPhone 11 Pro retails for $699 to $1,449 for the 512GB iPhone Pro Max. But if you add up the hard costs to make it, the price is significantly less.

According to a recent analysis by TechInsights and NBC News, it costs Apple roughly $66.50 for the battery. Then there's the triple camera module, which lets you take all of those beautiful shots. Those combined set Apple back about $73.50. The rest of the phone—a processor, the modem, and the memory, as well as the circuit boards that house them—goes for about $159. And a variety of other sensors, wires, PCBs, and so on are required to make the whole thing a phone you can hold in your hand. Those bits and pieces cost about $181. The total cost is about $490.50. So, why aren't iPhones cheaper?

Well, the price tag for a product like the iPhone also includes the cost of manufacturing and assembly, the expense of shipping the product to you, the software, marketing, and intangibles such as research and development costs.

You have to think of your content services in terms of your own bill of goods. Your following is not the only factor that determines your price. Pricing should also consider your niche, seasonal demand, your time, engagement rate, the deliverables, and the turnaround time the brand is requesting.

Whether you hire a photographer or have your friend take your photos, you should be charging for photography. If it costs you sixty dollars to hire a photographer for a brand campaign, you need to charge the brand the cost of photography in your price. Remember, time is *money*. It is valuable.

Now let's talk about industry standards so you know how to price and negotiate.

PRICING AND INDUSTRY STANDARDS

As we covered in Chapter 6, engagement rate matters. Highlighting a high rate will get you paid more. Brands spend hundreds to thousands on productions for promoting their products. They save a lot of money hiring micro influencers. They can afford to pay you what you are worth. If you have an engagement rate higher than the industry standard, you can earn more. Here are the benchmark rates:

- Micro: >15K ~ 3.86 percent
- Regular: 15K–50K ~ 2.39 percent
- Rising: 50K–100K ~ 1.87 percent
- Mid: 100K–500K ~ 1.62 percent
- Macro: 500K–1M ~ 1.36 percent
- Mega: 1M+ ~ 1.21 percent

The industry benchmark pay rate is around one hundred dollars per ten thousand followers on Instagram. But this is just a benchmark and does not factor in engagement, production, or your audience on additional platforms that you should charge for if you post there. Use benchmarks as a guide only. I say you don't get out of bed for less than $300 per campaign, unless it's a major brand like we discussed that will greatly advance your career just by affiliation.

If your engagement is higher than the industry average by at least 1 percent, increase your price and let a brand know why if they come back and attempt to negotiate a lower fee. You can increase your fee by 25-50 percent if you have higher engagement. There will likely be some negotiation on the brand side as well, but ultimately if you present a reasonable yet higher fee, the outcome will generally still be in your favor.

Many influencers make the mistake of charging what they think they can get versus *what the market will pay.* Usually, what we think people will pay is less than the industry rate. And following is not solely what determines your price. Other variables to consider are engagement rate, seasonal demand, and the time it will take to deliver a specific piece of content on top of the turnaround time a brand is asking for. Your price needs to be more than what the deliverables are worth.

Ask yourself: what is my hourly rate? Then, calculate how many hours it will take you to create and deliver the content and add that to the base price for what you are offering. Charging 10-15 percent more than what you feel comfortable with is an excellent rule to stick by. Though, don't be crazy. No one will pay you $10,000 if you have one thousand followers.

If you have a higher than average industry standard engagement rate, add this key comparison metric to your portfolio to show your engagement rate compared to the industry average. Marketing teams of large brands care about numbers, so always keep that top of mind. Do the math for them, and your higher price will be an easier sell. Also know that if you're an influencer in an oversaturated market like fitness, you might not be able to charge as much as someone who has niched down to, say, twenty-two-minute HIIT workouts for the busy professional.

Also, understand the power of seasonal demand and standard economics: high demand leads to higher rates. Take advantage of that and increase your seasonal holiday campaign rates. Many micro influencers are in high demand during the Christmas season, Black Friday, or other holidays like Valentine's Day. Follow the brands you love. Get on their email list. What are they promoting? What are they talking about?

Stories are generally an upcharge of 10–20 percent of your set rate. Charge more for sticker links or swipe-ups—even more than for a link in your bio—and additional highlights. That's an easy 20–30 percent upcharge, because stories are where the actual engagement is.

So, let's say you've been contracted by a brand to produce one Instagram post (a carousel of three images) and three Instagram stories for their upcoming new product launch campaign. They also want you to create outdoor content. Would you price yourself at $25 an hour? How about $35 or $50 an hour? Let's think this through. You will see you should be charging more than you think. Here are the steps you need to go through to deliver what the brand wants:

1. You spend an hour researching locations online and finally find the perfect spot for the shoot.
2. You don't have a go-to photographer yet, so you spend an hour researching photographers in your area. You DM a handful and get rates. Finally, you find the perfect person for your campaign.
3. You create a digital inspo board including shot styles from the chosen photographer and inspo shots from Pinterest, location looks, colors schemes, outfits, product shots, and a rough outline of your vision for the project. Then, you share it with the brand so everyone is on the same page. They provide feedback, and you adjust as needed. You also share this board with your photographer. They love you for doing this. It takes you two hours to do this.
4. You get your outfits together, steam everything, so it looks perfect. You spend a little extra time beautifying yourself for the camera so it takes anywhere from thirty minutes to two hours depending on your regime to get picture-perfect ready.
5. You drive to this location, find parking, and pay for parking. It takes thirty minutes. Parking costs fifteen dollars.
6. Your photographer for this shoot arrives on time. You both agree to a two-hour shoot and pay them sixty dollars per hour. You have two outfit changes and are constantly reviewing the shots the photographer is taking to ensure that it's the vibe you are going for. (It is the worst feel-

ing ever to get back photos that are not the best content possible because you and the photographer had different visions, so please do this.)

7. The photographer leaves but you stick around for another thirty minutes to get some sunset story videos. You were prepared, so you have your handy-dandy phone tripod. You film yourself talking into the camera or showing how the product is used.

8. You come home and decide to get some more stories inside your home because you want options to choose from. Also, you want to overdeliver an extra story or two to keep the brand wowed by you enough to re-sign you for a future campaign. This takes you an hour.

9. The next day you dedicate yourself to editing. You take thirty minutes to write a solid caption for your feed carousel. The photographer has already let you know they have a seventy-two-hour turnaround time, so you're ahead of the game. You know you may want to tweak the captions a little after reviewing the final images, but at least you have a general idea of what you want to say.

10. Next, you begin editing your stories. You create the text overlays and save the videos. You research relevant hashtags to push more reach. You use your Flick account to ensure your hash groups are on point. This takes you an additional hour.

11. The photographer delivers your edited content, you love it, and you pick your best three photos for your carousel. This takes you thirty minutes.

12. In an email, you send your photos with the caption, a video screen recording of your Instagram post draft, and downloads of your three Instagram stories (not posted yet) for the brand to approve and wait for their feedback.

13. The brand comes back and wants you to edit the caption with specifics they want mentioned and decide they don't like the filter you've used on the Instagram stories. You spend thirty minutes making these changes and resend for approval.

14. They approve. You're ahead of the game, so you're not scheduled to post for another two days.

15. You wait until your scheduled day, and you spend thirty minutes to one hour engaging with your audience before you post your branded content at your highest engaged hour. You engage in your DMs, like recent comments on your posts, respond to comments, go through your followers' list and most recent commenters, like their pics, and watch their stories. A couple stories grab your attention, so you send some engagement stickers.

16. You publish your approved content, and you spend one hour engaging with your audience on your new post.

17. You go about your busy day. Later you respond to every single comment on your post. You respond to every story and really push your love of the brand with your audience. You take screenshots of the best DMs you receive from your audience so you can share them with the brand when you provide your report in two days.

18. Before the twenty-four hours is up on your story viewing, you take screenshots of your insights for each story to share with the brand.

19. Two days later, you create a campaign report to share with the brand using a Canva template and all that does is go over your post insights you pulled directly from the post and your stories. You share some nice screenshots of DMs you received from your followers regarding the brand. You thank the brand for the opportunity, expressing how

much fun you had on this campaign and for your desire to work together in the near future.

20. You share your report PDF (DocSend link, ideally) via email, and within the body of your email you tell the brand your audience really loved learning about their product as they know it takes numerous touches with a brand for a follower to become a customer and you would love to further partner with them in this journey. You say you currently have availability for a longer-term partnership opportunity if they are interested in hearing more. They say yes!

21. You tell them about your three-month and six-month packages. They pick a package, and now you have a recurring client, and you are effectively building brand trust with your audience! Let's say they pass on a package for now. No stress! Reach back out in six weeks, remind them you've worked together in X month and you would love to see if they have any upcoming campaigns your audience would love. #winning

That is the process. As you can see, it takes time to produce a great campaign. Your price has to exceed just what you think your deliverables are worth. Your time and your brainpower have to be factored into your price. The brand is not just simply paying you for a carousel and some stories. Now, why would you ever accept anything unworthy of you?

You can present your rates as take it or leave it, but I don't recommend it if you have under 500,000 followers. Always be open to negotiation. If you take lower than your standard rate for your first campaign with a brand, kindly let them know that you'll take $200 this time but if you work together in the future the rate is $300.

PACKAGES AND PROPOSAL

Pitching packages in a proposal shows you're an influencer who is serious and a creative thinker. It's better than simply going to a brand with a rate. Think ahead before you enter conversations. Already have the number in your mind that you will be more than happy with, the number you will be satisfied with, and the disrespectful number you just walk away from.

Curate packages to pitch, not one-offs like a $400 post. Do not pigeonhole yourself into one post. Give brands a marketing strategy because that is actually what they need. It's so much more than about posting a photo. There's targeting involved and copy and creative planning. You are talking to large corporations, and they have the money. If they want to work with you, they will figure it out because you're saving these brands money. Professional photo shoots for creative advertising campaigns cost thousands of dollars.

Say a brand is considering you to promote its new leather jacket collection. You might go to them and say you'll post, provide three Instagram stories, and a Reel for $2,000. They might come back with a strict budget of $1,500. So then you take off the Reel, and you are still making more than if you pitched by placement, which maybe would have been $300 for one post.

Making more money from fewer deals is the way to go. Focus on content value at 80 percent organic, 20 percent promotions and collaborations, and that's a healthy balance. And if you want to do more partnerships, no stress, all you have to do is post more. The idea is that your feed is not all sponsored content. A high month could be 30, 35 percent is fine, but it's way too high if you get to 50/50. You will lose trust. People will see you are only connecting with them to make money. Same with brands. You want to build a long-lasting career, not just make a quick buck for six months and then lose all of your engagement and not be able to monetize anymore.

There are dozens of packages you can offer depending on your skillset. The easiest is the Instagram package—one post and three to five stories to complement it.

Business is all about relationships, so do your best work for them. The influencers I have seen that continuously earn a significant income consistently go a little above and beyond what they promise. Always add in more than what the contract requires. Show them you care about future success together. Add one post or one to two extra stories for free. It will cost you ten to fifteen minutes of extra time and guarantee they will become a returning customer—mo money, less future negotiation time.

Then, after a job well done, present the company with quarterly package opportunities. People need at least eight to ten touches with a brand before they think about purchasing, and companies know that. So take advantage of that upsell opportunity. If you have done a great job, they will want to work with you again too. Brands have customer journeys and know that one post from you won't be enough to recoup the money they spent hiring you. It takes time. Marketing representatives understand that there's a course and a flow and that to run an ad campaign costs them so much more if they have to get a new person into the funnel than it was two or five years ago. Your role as a micro influencer is not going away. Think long-term. If you can be that person for them and speak their language as a true marketer, you can build lasting relationships where you work with them more than once. So, at the end of the first partnership opportunity, request to go over the numbers to see if you can do additional monthly packages together because you believe in their brand and your people enjoy it. Share your experience with that brand continuously so that everyone can grow together.

Remember, you're never stuck at a price. Always raise your rates as you grow. Every five thousand followers equate to a 1–2 percent increase in engagement, so bump that price up accordingly.

If you need more help pricing yourself, join the Built to Influence community built2influence.com. All the support you need is available to you as a member of the community.

UPSELLS

Now you know to price as much as you can and offer them options to maximize the opportunity. Let's expand on that idea because you can do more to upsell. It's easy extra money.

It never hurts to ask if they want professional photos and access to a specific amount of edited photos during your negotiation. If so, that fee, for example, could be an additional $350. Or, perhaps you offer them a list of locations where you'll shoot within certain price ranges. Any time you can get a brand to pay for a shoot on location, do it. Send them three to four Airbnb or peer space locations to choose from if they are open.

Give them a fee up front and all it entails. You can either film and edit yourself or hire a professional. For instance: the price will be $5,000, including a rental venue for two hours, a photo shoot with 200 professional photos, 50 edited and 150 raws. But, whether you're paying someone to do this or you're doing it yourself, it's still a shit ton of work. You need to be compensated for doing the work and also arranging a shoot and showing up looking fab.

If they need content for their website or email campaigns or ads, those are upsells too. Maybe they love the photos you posted, and it was a carousel of five images. They ask to use them on their website. Awesome. You tell them that's going to be $2,000 for six months' usage. They will typically be cool with that because you are saving them money. And that brings us to usage rights.

USAGE RIGHTS

Know your usage rights so you don't get into a situation where you need to argue with a brand for using your photo somewhere other than the original agreed-upon post they paid you for. Brands pay you to share with your audience, not to use your content everywhere. Models know this because they make their money on usage, but a lot of influencers don't. Forgetting to charge for usage rights is how you lose a ton of money.

One influencer I know posted a picture of herself wearing a

famous brand like Roxy. They used her picture in a storefront, and she had no idea. When she found out she had grown to a point where she had management, they nipped that shit in the bud so quickly that she got paid. What the heck? She just didn't know. I can't tell you how often this happens. People frequently tag models in a commercial or billboard or marketing campaign that they didn't know about. That's when you send a cease and desist letter to get the money you are owed.

A brand that's new (or used to getting their way) will ask for total exclusivity. Cool, but no. Ask them to define how they would like to use your content and provide them with your rates for social channels, website, print, and email. Ask them where they would like to use your content, and then send them a particular package for those placements.

Stay away from charging the right to post on social media only and that should be included in your price. Unless you're over one million followers, it doesn't make sense to charge brands for what they came to you for, which is content they can use organically.

Be up front. Ask how the brand plans to use your image and video content. Companies require a license to use your content beyond the social media platform you've agreed on. Make sure you have a term in a contract that clearly defines usage, the amount of time you permit it, and which platforms you are allowing that content to be used on.

Brands might want to use your content for:

- Website banners
- In-store signage
- Billboards
- Mailers
- Bus wrappers
- Email content
- Ads from their account

Usage fees can and should be at minimum two to four times your standard post price, depending on your following and engagement rate. If you are still growing, do not overcomplicate it, simply double the rate because they are doubling the exposure.

As a professional self-marketer now, do not forget to ask if they will be using your creative for paid advertising. Always ask. If the brand's representatives say yes, charge for advertising rights. You have power as a creator. Brands make a shit ton of money—millions—on Facebook, Instagram, TikTok, Snapchat, and Pinterest ads using your UGC. So charge them for that right. Let them know you understand the power of UGC and that they'll make their investment back.

Here is a standard usage calculator to help you define your pricing:

- Brand website use: Your base rate + $300 – $500 per month of usage
- Brand ad use: Your base rate + $100 – $300 per month of usage
- Brand right to boost through your channels: Your base rate + $50 – $200 per month

Now, let's talk about exclusivity.

EXCLUSIVITY

If a brand is requesting you not to work with other brands during your contract duration, they must pay for that too, because you cannot accept new work during that period. If a brand representative comes to you and says they want to be the only jewelry company you work with for six months, calculate what you could be losing during that period. Suppose a brand like Kay Jewelers wants to pay you not to work with any other engagement ring brands while you work with them for six months—great, but you are losing out on money. You can come back to them and say that would be five grand per partnership, so they need to pay $15,000.

The key to this is to be reasonable. You're most likely not going to sign one every day or every month. But if you would be missing out on three or four contracts, have them pay for it.

GROW WITH INTENTION

Don't wait for the money to come to you. Go to the money. To build a megasuccessful career, you must produce content for as many high-traffic platforms as possible and sell opportunities for brands to engage with your audience on their behalf. Focus on Instagram, YouTube, and TikTok growth right now. That might change soon. Saturate those markets with your content. It will not only increase your following but also skyrocket your engagement and lead to additional upsells.

Keep your account worthy of engagement—honor the reason

your audience is there to engage with you and your life. Again, be sure to post no more than 20 percent sponsored content. Keep it around 15–18 percent if you can. People are not consciously following you to buy. They want to feel inspired and seen and informed. Always be working to increase your worth to brands.

BUILD STRATEGIC PARTNERSHIPS

Connect with other influencers and work with them to cross-promote. Influencers often make this so weird. It's not a competition. The faster you stop seeing it as one and learn to build partnerships with people and cross-promote, you're going to help each other out. It's one of the most innovative ways to grow.

Other influencers have similar communities where they have built trust. Say Meghan has five thousand followers, and they trust her, and so if she starts talking about you, they likely will buy because Meghan loves you. Now you're being intro-duced to an entirely new audience. They're getting introduced to someone new that they can aspire to be like.

The key is to not work with somebody who is barely seeing growth. That's a one-way relationship. You can be friends in the DMs, but don't approach them with some great marketing strategy if their engagement rate is less than yours. They have bad engagement for a reason.

Why would you want to promote someone who is getting an F when you're getting an A? Make sure the relationship is reciprocal. Also, be strategic with the products and services you choose to promote so you don't sacrifice the growth of your brand. Now, if it's a brand that has shitty engagement that you really believe in, well that's worth your time. And then, you are officially an asset that has higher than average negotiation power. They need you.

To this point, there are a couple of critical factors to keep in mind:

Only work within your related niche. Work with accounts whose goals and branding align with yours. Make sure you share similar audiences so their sponsorship resonates with your people.

Ensure partners are growing. Thoroughly review their account to see how many followers they're gaining each day. If they are gaining one hundred followers per day every week, it would be a great account to work with because they're going to be a lot bigger in a few weeks or months.

Regardless of whether they are a huge brand or not, losing thousands of followers a day might not be worth the collaboration unless it's well paid and provides elite exposure. Sometimes working with smaller, steadily growing brands is the best move.

Always view your potential deals from the frame of mind that what you are paid matters just as much as the potential engagement the brand you're working with provides you. This is why you see many influencers in the 200,000-300,000 range seemingly halting their growth. Yes, they are making larger, higher-earning partnerships, but they might not be making the best moves for their exposure.

Remember, you will experience a rut if you haven't yet. That's why it is essential to engage off the platform as well. Don't just wait for Instagram to grow you. Go grow yourself. A great way to do that is with PR.

EXPANDING YOUR BRAND WITH PR

PR is a powerful tool for micro influencers. Most people don't think to take advantage of the opportunity to reach out to the press. It is the perfect opportunity to share value with engaged audiences at scale.

Press is also the only way to get verified on Instagram. Have you ever seen someone who isn't famous with only 13,000 followers, but they are verified—an authority figure, a googleable name—and you think, *How?* Instagram shared this information recently: they have been published by high-ranking media outlets like *Forbes, Inc.,* or *Huffington Post.*

Micro influencers often guest-post for mid- to high-level online publications. Anyone can pay thousands of dollars to someone at *Forbes* to get in the sponsored content area or get their name in an article on *Business Insider* and similar publications. Typically, a person needs five pieces of high press. The only other way to be verified is to prove people are creating fake accounts in your name. Sometimes Instagram will verify you to protect other people from fraud.

To become verified, visit your account and click Request Verification. It takes you to a screen where it will ask you to define why you believe you are a public figure. From there, all you need to do is fill out a form in the app and link to the articles where you're published.

Reporters are *always* looking for a story from authority figures within a niche. Use this to your advantage. They need content. Always! And it's free to you. It just costs you time. So invest that time in getting published by pitching as much as possible. Follow up too. Editors, podcasters, reporters, bloggers all want to hear from you. It's their job to find and share exciting stories, and that's what you're going to give them.

The first time I was featured in *Forbes*, it was as a guest post. I reached out to someone in the business section when they were writing about influencers. I told them I'd love to speak on the topic because I work with influencers. They sent me questions, I provided feedback, and our collab piece was published.

So many frequently published thought leaders need content. Make it easy for them by pitching and writing with them. They are usually more than willing.

You might get more nos than yeses when you start, but that is okay. Pitch, learn, and adjust your pitch. Make it a constant practice. It can be time-consuming, which is why members of our Micro Influencer Academy get access to contacts and learn how to pitch to the media, but it does pay off royally.

PITCHING

Hey, I'm an influencer, and I want to stay at your hotel for free.

Does that sound like a persuasive pitch to you? Imagine you're a social media marketing representative for Omni Hotels and you receive a DM like this. Would you be inclined to DM back? How about if you received this instead:

> Hey, [Brand Contact Name], you have a beautiful hotel. I have read such wonderful things about it. I would love to stay and review your hotel to share it with my audience of millennial women in NYC who love to do staycations on the weekend. I know your property is one where they would love to stay.
>
> I would love to document my stay through my Instagram channel @username. Here's the link. I could share my experience through a series of Instagram stories and a post. I definitely want to highlight your incredible restaurant, which I have heard is not short of delicious. I've linked to some examples of content I have done for other hotels and travel partners. It would be great if I did a Reel because my reach is 5x higher for this placement. Let me know if this is of interest to you. Have a great day.

Which pitch was better? If you said the second one, bingo, you win. The first pitch has no allure to it. What's the payoff to the person receiving that message? It's very one-sided. You need to build a relationship.

When you engage, don't sound like everyone else. Approach brand representatives strategically, so you stand out as someone they would want to invest in. Make it about them, not about you, and keep DMs short and sweet. And only reach out to people where you've formed a connection. Do not ask for anything until you nurture a brand relationship for at least thirty days. Brand representatives could see you as greedy versus someone who cares about their products or services. After thirty days, you can pitch. And that first pitch should be:

> Hi, [brand name], I am a huge fan of [SPECIFIC PRODUCTS or collection]! Can you connect me with the person who handles influencer partnerships? I would love to see if any of your upcoming projects would be a good fit for my audience.

They will respond with an email address and a name and then you reach out to that person with a more detailed pitch where you share your desire to promote that is similar to the one above. Do not price drop or include your media kit until they have requested it.

If they ask for your pricing up front, ask them to share a bit about their upcoming projects. What is their creative vision for their next influencer partnership? See what they say and then you pitch. Send a project proposal based on what the brand wants. Angle your content to meet the brand's needs. For instance, you might suggest one Reel featuring you outside in the city wearing the jacket, close-up and zoomed-out action shots, and six stories where you praise the make and quality of the jacket and share your discount code with your audience. End the proposal with your total cost for the project. Never line item cost per placement for Reels, static posts, and carousel stories.

If they say the price is too high, ask them if they would like to remove three stories and you can drop the price $500. If they say yes then you've negotiated and made way more. Now you're not charging only $300 for a single Reel based solely upon your follower count.

So Social has signed almost all our megacelebrity clients via cold email and DM outreach. We understand how to speak to brands and influencers and can get deals done. We offer dozens of email and DM templates to Micro Influencer Academy Members, so it's as easy for people as possible.

Track all of your reach-outs to brands (press too). Remember, data is everything. Know your conversion rate. How many reach-outs were successful? How many didn't respond or said not at this time? Track the initial reach-out date to the date a contract is signed, and it will help you understand your sales cycle. We teach you how to effectively do this in the academy.

PITCHING SUCCESS TIPS

According to brands and successful influencers alike, less is more. Aim for no more than two pages. When pitching brands through influencer marketing platforms, use your portfolio with broad price ranges. Never set a price.

When pitching a brand via DM and email, do not start the conversation with pricing, as the brand will always try to get the best deal possible. Maintain as much negotiation power as possible.

The purpose of sending in an initial pitch is to get them to ask for your media kit. The one should show how fabulous you are with your stats, platforms, creativity, testimonials, and not your pricing. When you put prices for various types of content off the bat, they will likely come back with a budget of half the amount and you will lose all negotiation power.

Do your research instead and put together a proposal package for that brand if they are interested in working with you. Give them one price for specific deliverables and a creative scope of work. When you present a price by package and a brand comes back with a lower offer, simply remove a service from your proposal to make that amount work. Whenever possible, ask for specifics of what they need and let the brand representatives share their vision for the project. Here is how to do that:

Hi, [Brand Name], I have been a fan of your brand for a while. Product A is one of my favorites. Do you have any upcoming projects you'd like influencer promotions for?

If they respond *yes*, ask more about the project regarding deliverables, the scope of work, and budget. If they ask you first what your price is for a particular scope of work, mark up the number by 15–20 percent, because they will talk you down in most cases.

An example offer you could pitch a brand is:

- One Instagram in-feed image
- Three Instagram stories (nine frames)
- One Facebook post
- One promotional Reel
- Final Rate: $2,000 (your desired price)

When you send your media kit and brand proposal, it should include your pricing and a brief outline of the creative concept for each piece you suggest to create. Always send documents of this nature through DocSend or a similar platform where you can track who reviewed them. It's a great way to control what information is out there about you. Also, you can always delete a link to a media kit or update your metrics, offers, and package pricing without sending a new link. Also you will never have missed information floating around the internet about your business. Lastly, with media kits and proposals, always include an offer to hop on a call to discuss further.

If you take a lower offer than your presented proposal, let them know you are and ask for an exchange in return like cross-promotion on their channels or your favorite product valued at a specific amount from their store. Know and act from your worth, and you will score big. Just remember, the power is always in the follow-up and negotiation.

FOLLOW-UP AND NEGOTIATION

If you DM a brand and they are interested, they will send you a social media manager's email address. Then you'll send the powers that be your brand praises, your soft pitch, and your media kit with no pricing. Maybe they love it, so they ask for pricing. At this point, you ask for specifics: *What are you looking for?* They want a Reel for their new fall collection. So then you get together your proposal—a nicely put-together package from a platform like Canva—that outlines your strategy. You will do a Reel where you're wearing five outfits with a series of photos of you posing in Times Square. You'll include a few stories as well, for a price of $2,000.

At this point, the representative typically will not respond immediately. What the heck? You think they passed on you.

Wait a few days, maybe a week, then follow up. You don't want to be annoying or look desperate. Don't let a week go by though—by then, if you haven't heard back, send a check-in: *Hey, do you have any questions? Would love to hop on a call to discuss further.*

Imagine she has received hundreds of offers at this point that she needs to go through. Her team needs to review multiple metrics and the campaign they are launching. They are busy, and you are not their only focus. You have no idea where they are. You have no idea what their process of choosing influencers for their upcoming campaigns is like. Very rarely is a team picking only one person. It might be you and three or four other influencers that they have the budget for in that quarter. You are not top of mind.

Never send a PDF to anybody. Use DocSend to upload and track your PDF so you know who looked at it, how long they looked at it, and what pages they reviewed. That way you'll know if they have reviewed the pricing. It happens all the time that they haven't gotten to it. Maybe they read the first page, then had to jump into a meeting. It happens. By using DocSend you can follow up with, *Were you able to review my portfolio?* You can also say with full disclosure that you have DocSend and can see that they haven't read the second page yet. You can tell them that's where it gets good. Remind them to check it out and let you know if they have any questions. At which point, you will look very strategic and business-minded. These are qualities they are seeking. But make sure you don't hound them for opening your portfolio. They are busy. Always take that perspective when sending a message like this. Also, DocSend allows you to update a doc without having to resend. So you can update your portfolio whenever you need to, or revise with new pricing whenever without having to reach back out to brands.

It is wiser for an influencer to set themselves apart by bringing ideas to brand marketers. Think about how weird it is to meet someone on the internet. This is like asking a stranger to pay you a decent amount of money in full faith. So, overexplain your strategy. Put it in a sleek proposal, not in written form in an email. This is especially true if you are asking for more. Otherwise, a brand wouldn't know why they are paying you $2,000. Explain the project. Come with a vision for the project; you want to prove you are worth good money. And remember, your job is to be creative.

The biggest deals are done on the phone, so any time you can get on the phone with a brand, do it. Always include a call to action in your proposal to hop on Zoom. When you can get them on the phone, you are pitching them in person. You get to walk them through your vision and get instant feedback. It can turn into a wonderful brainstorming session.

About 99 percent of the time, a brand that wants to work with you will negotiate your rate, especially if you don't have a very large following. Always go through this checklist of questions:

- What are the requested deliverables?
- What will it cost to complete this project?
- How much time will it take you to complete this project?
- What is the requested timeline for this project?

- What is the minimum compensation you are willing to accept for this project?
- What is your *hell yeah* goal compensation for this project?

Be sure to sit with yourself and answer these questions before negotiating.

If a brand reaches out to you with a specific offer, *always* counter. They came to you, so don't be afraid to negotiate. Don't fear they will go to the next influencer. *They came to you.* Of course, it's up to you to decide whether you will negotiate or not, but I highly recommend you do.

Continue to learn and master how to negotiate effectively and how to frame a conversation. To do that, you need to understand that brand's why. My best advice is to listen more than you talk.

Understand their pain points and overall desires with this deal. What problem will working with you solve for them? The dance of negotiation isn't about getting what you want solely. It's also about ensuring that the company gets what they want and need, which is great content and exposure at a fair price. So, don't be afraid to walk if the offer is disrespectful to you, especially if you have done previously successful paid brand work. Sometimes the shoe does not fit, and that is okay. Know your worth. Listen to your gut. If it doesn't feel right to you, it's not.

Also, decide on what you want ahead of time. Know your numbers. Know the terms you're willing to accept. Know the value of what you're getting and what you will provide. But also really focus on brands that you can build a sustainable recurring business relationship with.

Rob Massar is an entertainment and business law practice owner in Los Angeles, servicing talent, creatives, and emerging companies, who I've been blessed to work with. As a native Angeleno, he told me he'd been exposed to exceptional art, talent, and performers. But it wasn't until he worked as a talent scout for the Chicago Cubs and New York Yankees that he understood the mindset of world-class talent. From the boardroom to the ball field, performance is about fundamentals, preparation, and mindset. Because of his experience and ability to nurture talent, he's made it his mission to give people peace of mind for their pursuit. Massar says before any negotiation, think ahead. There are three points to consider:

1. ZOOM OUT

You must understand the landscape of your industry as a whole to negotiate contracts effectively. What is the market rate for your services? Are back-end royalties or other forms of compensation standard? Will expenses be reimbursed?

2. KNOW YOUR FLOOR

At what point are you comfortable walking away from the deal because you are being grossly undervalued?

3. DETERMINE MOTIVATIONS

Negotiations are all about understanding motivations and leverage. So, ask yourself: What are your motivations for the deal? What are the other party's motivations? Why are they "at the table," and what do you provide that they can't get from someone else? In essence, what is your "actual value" (services you will provide) and what is your "perceived value" (why they value you in particular)?

The best advice I have ever been given around negotiation is to take the emotion out of the situation. When the decision is objective, not emotional, and feels personal, you won't get hung up on winning or losing. You'll just calmly work toward getting the best deal you can, which will ultimately lead you to a successful close.

And remember, it's okay to say no. Embrace the advice of influencer Gigi Robinson @itsgigirobinson. "Don't get hung up. Just move on. It's not that serious. It's just not right now," she says.

After you have some wins under your belt—hell, even before—remember you're not going to say yes to everything! Ask yourself whether this partnership serves your six-month, one-year, or three-year goals. Score as many long-term contracts as you possibly can. These are highly sought after and very exclusive, and way more valuable to both parties. Always look at every brand deal like it's a potential ongoing relationship, which also means being smart about the contracts you sign. We'll cover that in Chapter 8.

DO THIS NOW:
- Start pitching. Put together packages so you stand out and look professional.

- What can you do to upsell? Consider this and add upsells to your packages.
- Follow the guidance in this chapter to pitch like a master.
- Do not forget about usage rights and exclusivity. Brands need to pay you to use your content in other ways than what you agree upon for social media.

CONTRACTS & LEGAL

"Let's write our story and sing our song, let's hang our pictures on the wall."

—SHAWN MENDES

How awful would it be to do all this work and not get paid? Before you do any work, make sure you have a binding contract. You're a CEO now. No great businessperson does work on their word without an agreement in writing.

It does not matter how big a brand is. Never do work without a signed contract. If you do, the company is not legally obligated to pay you. *Always* ask for a contract to review and get it signed by both parties. The deliverables must be in writing.

Inexperienced influencers who do not treat their platform as a business might sidestep a contract. Please know there are bad apples in every tree. There's always going to be someone out there who will take advantage of anything new, hot, and trending. And at this moment, that is micro influencers.

It's you. There are scams. There are people who are pretending to be large brands. It's not hard for anyone to create an online presence that looks like a legitimate company. And it's not hard to attract them. If a company does not offer an agreement and tells you to send your PayPal address or billing address to wire money, that is a red flag. Never give out your account number.

Do your due diligence. Never immediately assume any company is legit. Make sure they have products that you can order. There are many ambassador scams too, where brands create ambassador programs that do not pay but say they will. They might say they'll pay you "like 40 percent of everything," and you think that's a sweet deal. Is it? Do your research and ask for the contract.

Many inexperienced influencers assume that major brands will pay them when they are ready to collect. If you don't have a contract in place with specifics on timing and based on what deliverables, deals can go sideways after you've done the work. Big brands are negotiating major deals all the time too. If you're not Kim Kardashian, it could take months to pay you if the payout is not in writing. It's not personal, but you're not the priority. Oftentimes, their vendor payout period is four to six weeks out. So ask questions and negotiate those terms whenever possible. Have terms in writing so they can't push off payment. Also, make sure you have their legal business address, a point of contact for their accounting department, and the company's tax ID number to know it is a real business.

I am always wary of influencers working with people who are

starting brands that are not legally real. If something goes wrong, who are you suing?

Members of our Micro Influencer Academy get access to our contract template that our attorney who works with many high-level creators and entrepreneurs created for our influencer students. You can edit this template where you define the deliverables and payment terms. Often, this contract is far better than what their company gives you, which makes you look professional. You can also use your friendly neighborhood Google to find micro influencer contracts. Pick one that makes sense to you that you can clearly understand.

If at all possible, have an attorney review the contract. Maybe you have a family friend who is an attorney. Hit them up. Or use an inexpensive contractor through Upwork. There are attorneys all over the world that are not very expensive by the hour. Never get all excited and sign your life away. It's worth the extra set of eyes.

How do you know how to negotiate and what terms are appropriate to ask for? Rob Massar also has three rules for micro influencers heading towards a negotiation:

1. HOLD YOURSELF ACCOUNTABLE

Hold yourself to the same expectations as someone you would hire. Think about the person you would hire to represent you or your company. How would you want them to conduct themselves? What would their daily tasks be? Would they be prompt to meetings? What expectations would you have of them?

While these are just a few of the questions to review, making a list of clear, manageable expectations will give you achievable benchmarks. You can then celebrate small victories and hold yourself accountable. Remember, you are human and thus fallible. So, you don't need to be perfect. But you do need to be accountable.

2. BE OBJECTIVE

Most businesses, such as LLCs or corporations, are separate legal entities from their owners. They have different bank accounts, addresses, and IRS tax IDs (employer identification numbers a.k.a. EINs). Even as a sole proprietor, you should separate the "professional you" from the "personal you." It's so important because our emotions can cloud our judgment.

Like the accountability exercise above, Massar asks clients how they would like a hired rep to make decisions on their behalf. They say, "Calculated, objective, purposeful, or businesslike." So, be objective, ask for advice, and look at the industry's status as a whole to put the deal into context.

3. RESPECT YOURSELF

Respect yourself, your talent, and your worth. If you are "sitting at the table," you deserve that opportunity. Negotiating against yourself or taking a lesser deal because you want to be easygoing is self-limiting. The person on the other side of the table is also running a business; they are trying to cut corners and costs. People will respect you if you stand up for yourself. Jay-Z said it best: "I'm not a businessman. I'm a business, man." #hellyeah. I love that.

These are your considerations heading into any business discussion. Then the golden rule again is: always have a signed contract. If they don't have a contract, send one. If I've said this a few times, there is a reason for it. Do not not have a contract.

Influencers serious about scaling their careers should consult an attorney for specific business contracts when they get into the thousands. Eat the cost. It will be worth it. It's easy to graze over detail in a contract. When your eyes aren't trained for legal speak, an attorney doesn't hurt.

WHAT TO LOOK OUT FOR

Before you sign a contract, review it, always. Read the entire contract, and review with an attorney whenever possible. You will likely sign a vendor agreement, a statement of work (SOW) and a W-9. Read everything, even if it is a hundred pages long! Understand that contract front to back. Ask questions to gain clarity when needed. Review the deliverables thoroughly to make sure you agree.

Understand the payment terms. Generally, you will not get paid right away. Usually, you will be paid within thirty to sixty days after you have delivered work. Remember exclusivity rights to ensure it is a fair deal. Make sure the agreement doesn't keep you from working with other related brands. You are building a career in one specific niche. Make sure the company isn't keeping you from working with competing brands. Don't sign an unfavorable contract. Constantly renegotiate if need be.

Get the following in writing:

- Scope of work
- Amount per post
- Types of posts
- Usage rights
- What are the platforms where you'll post?
- Permission to edit content?
- Days or dates you will post
- The subject matter of the content and caption
- Is it product or brand specific or both?
- Terms specific to end date or is this ongoing?
- Length of videos or blog posts or resolution and dimensions
- The legal name of the business (not their Instagram name) and its address (you should also provide the same)
- Payment terms and expectations of payment
- Where the brand is allowed to post your content
- How long your content is permitted to remain active on their socials, site, print, or emails

Deliverables. Clearly understand what content you're being asked to create and deliver, including the format it should follow (i.e., Instagram posts, carousels, stories, etc.), the number of posts, which platforms the content will be shared to, and the posting schedule. The more you have to create, the more you should be paid.

Usage. How a brand uses your image and distributes sponsored content can make or break a brand deal, especially if they're seeking to do these things in perpetuity (a.k.a. forever). Many brands distribute sponsored content on affiliate company platforms and do so beyond social media and the internet. Much consideration should be given to this provision to ensure your rights as a creator are protected. Also, make sure you're adequately compensated for such asks.

Exclusivity. No brand wants you to work with competitors during the term of your contract with them. However, be sure that this provision is specific and limited in time, so you aren't missing out on other lucrative deals and that you're adequately compensated for more extended exclusivity periods.

Casey Handy-Smith, who is the founder and managing attorney at C. Handy Law, a premier contract law firm for influencers, entertainers, and creative entrepreneurs, says so many creatives are thrown when they see terms that seem overreaching. They automatically think they're being taken advantage of when they aren't. Brand negotiations will always get the best deal, especially with influencers who don't have representation. "If you aren't afraid to negotiate and demand higher compensation for that tad-too-long exclusivity provision, it doesn't have to be a red flag that stops you," Handy-Smith says.

Whenever possible, ask brands for creative examples of work they would like you to emulate for this partnership because it will save you so much hassle. The brand and influencer often have two different visions. Make sure you are clear, and the representative you are dealing with is clear.

Don't be afraid to send a contract back and request revisions. You are not a brand partner until both parties sign the contract. The deal is never done until both parties sign the contract! If they agree to pay you your asking price, it's a win-win for everyone.

DELIVERING YOUR WORK

The agreement includes an SOW—a scope of work. An SOW is an outline that details your entire creation process and when the deliverables are expected. If you're not familiar, google "SOW templates," and you can easily find an editable download that meets your needs.

An SOW ensures all parties are on the same page regarding deliverables and the creative the brand is seeking. It helps you avoid situations where you produce content brand representatives don't love. I've worked with brands where it happens. It is hugely underwhelming as a marketer to receive content from an influencer that is just plain shitty and not on par with what is paid. Make sure brand representatives review your work before posting. Offer a campaign review four to seven days before it goes live.

Major issues can arise where a contract has been signed but the influencer's posts are not what the company wants. It might turn into a dispute, and they might not pay. It's an unspoken industry standard to share the deliverables before they're posted. Everybody has a different definition or visual definition of what content should be. If you deliver a moody and dark photo of you drinking a latte and the brand is all beach vibes and happiness, they're not going to like that. You never want to post without a brand's consent. Give the company options to review, and always overdeliver.

Even before you create content, you can provide them with a strategy and a mood board, so creatives with the company align with your course of action. (Platforms like Canva have great mood board templates you can easily edit that look professional.) It will also help you deliver better creativity because you have clarity. Maybe you will use a sepia-tone color scheme. Or wear a particular outfit. It's better to over-explain or overshare than underdeliver. You are a business providing a service. You are a representative of this brand. Approach all you do from this perspective.

Even if a brand gives complete creative freedom, explain your process. It will guarantee clearer communication and expectation from the brand. Include details of where you want to shoot, the lighting, the color schemes, the filters, and presets you're thinking about using. Make it clear which hashtags and words you will use to disclose this is a paid sponsorship your audience is seeing. Be open to opinions before you work to understand what may not be on par with the vision. You never want to walk into a situation where you're not being paid, or you never get work again with a company or related brand—because marketing representatives talk.

Deals also need to follow current Federal Trade Commission (FTC) guidelines concerning endorsements and testimonials in advertising. Double-check those in case the brand isn't doing its due diligence. Google them. They change often, so always protect yourself.

Not understanding payment terms is a big mistake influencers make. Everyone thinks they're going to be paid immediately, or 50 percent up front and the rest immediately after. Nope, you're a vendor. Large corporations have payment schedules that you need to be aware of. It could take three to six weeks after you deliver to get paid. Read that fine print to understand their payment schedule. Most brands are open to negotiating. It's not always in their favor to pay you immediately. They wait to see the success rate first and your content. If it wasn't quality, they might take longer to pay you.

There is one platform called Lumanu that allows influencers to get paid faster by being the middleman. Brands pay them, and they pay you, and it's faster. So always check if they use Lumanu and get on there to make your life easier.

In the end, take the advice of Handy-Smith, who says to do your homework and build community. Thanks to the internet, there are so many resources available to help influencers navigate the industry's business side. There's no excuse to walk into any deal completely blind. The key, however, is finding and using credible resources from experts. That's where your community comes into play. Tap into those around you who are a few steps ahead. Don't be afraid to ask for help. With contracts in place, you will save yourself from much insanity.

DO THIS NOW:

- Do you have your own contract that you can provide to brands? Get one immediately or join our academy to get access to our bulletproof brand partnership template.
- Read every contract before you sign it. Know what you are agreeing to.
- When in doubt, seek advice from an attorney.

CHAPTER 9

THE SHITTY REALITIES
OF SOCIAL MEDIA

"Be good to everyone. You never know who might be suffering alone."

— MARKIPLIER

The influencer profession does not come with a safety manual, though perhaps it should. Social media is the primary tool, and like any tool, there are dangers around using it. The influencer industry can be very rewarding but mentally challenging too.

Social media is an endless parade of information that's a combination of the practical (how to write a book) and less useful tidbits, depending on who you ask (like your friend's cappuccino art that morning), delivered to the palm of your hand. It's a strange and wonderful medium that gives people access to a menu of on-demand information that spans the world. It is a wonderful tool packed with daily affirmations, stats, and skill sharing. But also, it's a place friends and family offer advice without being asked. People engage in conversations around trivial topics that can be cognitively draining, but at the same time, they feel unable to avoid them. Social media is a real paradox.

It is interesting for me to work with influencers but not necessarily be one myself. I have a perspective where I get their world, understand what they deal with, and get a behind-the-scenes look at their experience. The influencer role can be amazing but also intensely stressful. It can cause a person to be overly obsessed or disconnected from reality.

I would lose sleep if I didn't fully address the mental health realities that being an influencer on any social media platform can bring. You must know that before you invest any more time into this career. Because you are your product, it is easy as an influencer for your life and work to collide more than most people's.

With this final chapter, my intention is to be proactive to help influencers avoid burnout and mental health crises. Honestly, I see it way too much. So, please, protect your mental health as your top priority, always. It is a serious priority for me. I want you to win, yes, but I want you to win in the healthiest headspace possible.

By nature, we are social creatures, which is why we are drawn to social media. However, social media use has been linked to an increased risk of depression, anxiety, loneliness, self-harm, and suicidal thoughts. Social media can exacerbate an experience of FOMO that snowballs. The more a person sees others doing what they aren't, the more they feel left out, which can lead to more scrolling.

In 2019, in an article released by *The Guardian* titled "How Instagram Takes a Toll of Influencers' Brians," fashion influencer, Alexandra Mondalek, explained how social media can be too close and convenient. Influencers often develop relationships with their phones or computers where they can't stop. I have seen this happen to many influencers. Mondalek says, "It's the rat-race lifestyle boiled down into the palm of your hand, and sometimes it feels inescapable.".

It's also been suggested that micro influencers have a higher tendency to develop anxiety and depression. Many are still at the beginning of their careers and constantly comparing themselves to others. Comparison can kill personality and rob you of your greatness and purpose. However, there is some good news on this front. Researchers found that influencers and audience alike are less likely to feel put down by content they relate to when it's been posted by a celebrity versus a micro influencer. For instance, a mixed-race woman in a middle-class home will feel more encouraged seeing another woman like her achieving dreams that seem out of reach.

For this chapter, I interviewed several doctors and mental health experts who are also social media influencers for their perspectives and strategies on how to run a successful influencer business that doesn't drive you insane or lead to burnout. The consensus was that social media is a tool, and like any tool, it can be used in good or bad ways. "Every human invention has the potential to be used for harm or good," says

Dr. Courtney Tracy, a licensed clinical social worker, doctor of clinical psychology, and clinical entrepreneur.

Dr. Courtney @the.truth.doctor, has a YouTube show and podcast, *The Truth Doctor Show*, that reaches over 3.5 million people every month. When I asked her if she thought social media was doing more harm than good, she said no. She said it depends on how people use social media. "Do they use it to connect on a deeper level, or to avoid deep connection...to inspire themselves, or as the main source of their low self-esteem...are they kind on social media, or are they cruel?"

Dr. Courtney said social media *has* caused us to connect more. Still, there is absolutely the need for safety and security regulations around bullying, harassment, misinformation, and other harmful aspects of social media. "It is less of a social media problem and more of a human society problem," she told me.

Divija Bhasin, a counseling psychologist with a double master's in clinical psychology, is an influencer @awkwardgoat who creates lighthearted content to spread awareness about mental health. She raised similar arguments. "Social media has led to the accessibility of more information for millions of people who might not have been aware without it," said Bhasin.

Apart from awareness, Bhasin also said it's a great way to make a career for creatives. It has further made having a small business easier for people of all age groups. She has witnessed so many people become financially independent from the comfort of their homes, even during a pandemic.

The influencer career has certainly allowed many people to have better mental health and experience more fulfillment in life in many cases.

Influencers own their time. They can choose to take a day off if they need to without a doctor's note. Influencers like Gigi Robinson @itsgigrobinsion are using social media to have a career that's better for their health. "One inclination to become an influencer was I was burning out at my job because I live with a chronic illness," she said.

Gigi struggled to work a full-time job. She was at the doctor frequently, which was a major predicament for her. She also saw how many people struggled with nine-to-five culture and how real burnout is in the corporate world.

Unfortunately, that can happen as an influencer too. The first step of counteracting the effects of social media is recognizing the common pitfalls and then taking actions to care for yourself so you don't end up burnt out, sick, or needing to stop altogether to save you from yourself.

THE THREE MOST COMMON INFLUENCER MIND F*CKS

Social media releases dopamine, which is one of the brain's pleasure hormones. When you're scrolling through social media you get the same brain buzz you would when you have sex, eat your favorite meal, or drink a glass of vino. But what makes it even more addictive is the inconsistent nature of the apps.

Our brains are wired to pursue pleasurable outcomes. With

social media, there is always the chance of a reward, though it does not guarantee it. Think of a time you're scrolling through Reels on TikTok. Maybe you watch a weird prank video of an ex-girlfriend blindfolding a dude and surprising him because she flew across the world to profess her love and get back together. But it's a scenario you've seen before. So you think, *Whatever*, and keep scrolling. The next video might be a dancing cat and dog dressed like a salt and pepper shaker from @animalsdoingthings and it's hilarious. Any minute while scrolling you could get that dopamine buzz you didn't even realize you were searching for, so you just keep scrolling. The same brain response happens in gambling addicts.

It's no wonder that according to an article published by HelpGuide.org, "Social Media and Mental Health," which profiled one study conducted by the University of Pennsylvania, people on Facebook, Instagram, and Snapchat had increased feelings of loneliness that decreased with less use.

In my experience, the top challenges influencers face are:

1. Becoming overly obsessed with metrics and the online world
2. Struggling with body image, comparison, and the need to look good
3. Overcoming the assumption that being an influencer is easy

The first step is recognizing the common pitfalls and then taking actions to care for yourself so you don't end up burnt out, sick, or needing to stop altogether and get a new career.

So this chapter offers some simple tips to overcome the mental challenges of being an influencer.

PITFALL #1: BECOMING OVERLY OBSESSED WITH METRICS AND THE ONLINE WORLD

Too many influencers are overly obsessed with their metrics. They might think, *My engagement rate went down. People don't like my content. Or my followers hate me.* I have seen influencers being super hard on themselves for no logical reason.

You can do everything right but still have a shitty day or week, or month. Instagram can change its algorithm, and it messes everything up for a few weeks. There are so many factors out of your control. Remember that you just don't know what's going on behind the scenes. At Instagram, they are split testing things on the platform that are going to mess with your engagement rates, with how people engage with new content.

You can't take business to heart. If your engagement is down, there are so many strategies to bring it back up. Maybe you're not posting as much as you used to. Or you're testing new content, but it doesn't work on the platform anymore. Maybe you're posting too much branded content. There are so many what-ifs. But anything is also possible. You could post a Reel that goes viral the next day.

PITFALL #2: STRUGGLING WITH BODY IMAGE, COMPARISON, AND THE NEED TO LOOK GOOD

One article from HelpGuide.org, "Social Media and Mental Health," reported that many people feel inadequate in their appearance, and although they know social media is fake, it makes them feel worse about insecurities.

Another survey from Inzpire.me showed how 32 percent of influencers said their job gave them a negative body image. Forty-seven percent felt their job had such a negative impact on their mental health they had to leave.

It's human nature to want to be loved, respected, and admired and that is exactly what social media exacerbates. If you pay close attention you'll see it daily. Influencers often post about how the platform magnifies their deepest physical and mental insecurities. It's beautiful when they do share these moments because it reminds us that we aren't crazy when we feel this way on the platform too. It's okay to humanize the realities of the platform. It's actually important because posting a too-polished life perpetuates the problem.

In 2020, an article published by *Psychology Today* titled "Social Media Affects Influencers' Mental Health," outlined how many influencers feel a constant pressure and comparison to other people in their niche. Many end up feeling like they're portraying a false reality or embellishing. It's reasonable to assume many influencers have imposter syndrome and feel major pressure to live the life people think they have. This can absolutely increase anxiety, depression, and unhappiness. Influencers can easily feel like they are not enough.

You have to go into the platform every day with the mentality that there are facts and there is truth. There are plenty of reasons to feel insecure when you tap open social media apps. That is a fact. However, the truth of the matter is, you are not your insecurities. The truth is there are too many moments and connections to nurture, inspire, and untangle and grow the beauty, passion, and purpose that is within you, as well. Be you! When you find yourself comparing, remember that a crayon doesn't look at a pencil and think, *Man, I'm not sharp enough*, any more than a pencil looks at a crayon and thinks, *I am not colorful enough*. Each tool has its purpose. The more you stay focused on you and your lane, the more successful you will be. I guarantee it. No one can do you as well as you can; tap into your power.

PITFALL #3: OVERCOMING THE ASSUMPTION THAT BEING AN INFLUENCER IS EASY

Many people think being an influencer is an easy job when first starting. It's not. It's going to require a lot of you. There are also many mental health professionals who don't fully get the world of influence yet, so when a patient shows up for help, while their doctor is trained and very smart, they might miss really understanding that person's world.

There will most likely be haters, bullies, and seasons in your career in which you feel it's not even worth pursuing. Cyberbullying does happen and although it's wrong, you have to learn to not let the haters ruin your day. They don't know your truth. It's helpful to remember the old adage, "Hurt people hurt people." It's 100 percent true. When you can get to a place where you empathize with their inner suffering more than you take offense, that is a powerful position you hold online. Don't let any hater win. You are always in control of how you let others make you feel.

Remember your worth, my friend, and why you started. What

is your why? Lean into that. And when you feel like you need to check your mental health, remember the habits that are good for you and your resilience.

PRINCIPLES FOR INFLUENCER MENTAL RESILIENCE

Living by four basic tenets will keep your mental health in check. You've got to:

1. Think abundantly
2. Take time off social
3. Extinguish hate with perspective
4. Set personal boundaries

These four structures will keep you in a healthy state of mind. They may seem straightforward, but it never hurts to have more advice or at least a reminder. Sometimes doing what we should requires a kick in the butt from a friend.

HEALTHY HABIT #1: THINK ABUNDANTLY

Instead of being super down, get curious. Whatever the problem, see it as a business problem you need to solve. That's it. Remember, it's a massive platform. There are billions of people on Instagram. And you don't need to feel like you're competing with any of them. Become friends with them. Learn from them.

"Reach out to people in the same profession and create a support network since they might understand your problems more than the people who aren't creators," said Bhasin. If you're a beauty blogger and have an account and see another beauty blogger, become friends online. Engage with their content. Genuinely, you're not against each other. You can help each other grow your accounts because you have the same niche and the same expertise to talk about. How wonderful would that be to talk to someone who understands precisely where you are at and how you feel about the platform? Don't take your perceived competitors for granted. It's a job, but it's also fun.

It's helpful to remind yourself to stay in your lane. Everyone is on their journey at different points too. What do you need to do to get to the next level?

Dr. Courtney suggests focusing on content that you like and what your audience wants to see. "If you aren't being yourself fully, you will burn out trying to be something you're not," she said.

Bhasin also encourages influencers to unfollow pages that don't make them feel good. "Everyone's niche and growth will be different...healthy comparison is good, but everyone grows at their own pace."

It's okay to unfollow, and also, to take time away.

HEALTHY HABIT #2: TAKE TIME OFF SOCIAL

Scheduling time away from the platform is crucial for your mental health, especially when it's your job. For me, I cap it at like nine o'clock—no more DMs or looking for new clients after that time. I do not do work outside of the time that I've allotted for it. So, turn it off. Most people have dedicated work hours. Do not spend thirteen hours on a platform. It affects how you see yourself. It affects how you see other people. It affects how you see the world. You don't want to have a negative relationship with your job.

Social media is nice to consume as a person, but you have to cap the hours that you're on those platforms as an influencer. It's a synthetic form of reality where people are constantly being fed polished, manipulated content.

Dr. Courtney said influencers lose the ability to pursue social media for fun so they need to put the phone down when they are not working. "Our brains activate the same way on the app whether we are working or just scrolling for fun," she said.

She suggests having a private family and friends and fun account only to create a healthy separation between work and personal life. And it's good advice, because research has shown that in-person eye contact with a person you admire lowers the risk of depression.

HEALTHY HABIT #3: EXTINGUISH HATE WITH PERSPECTIVE

When you are in a somewhat superficial industry like the entertainment industry—I have so much respect for those guys—there is an unrealistic amount of pressure put on you. The number of eyes on you as an influencer can be absurd. People who don't know you at all will have all the opinions in the world about you. If anybody tells you to get over it or that you're a baby, you're not. It's a lot of pressure.

Any influencer receiving or who has received hate needs

a support system to balance the negative with the positive. "Our brains listen more to the negative because [our brain] thinks we need to know it to be better," said Dr. Courtney. She also said online is rarely ever meant to help you be better. It's meant to make you feel bad.

You're doing a very difficult job that most people say they want, but they probably wouldn't want if they were in it and realized the amount of resilience it takes for a person to succeed in this space. People you don't know will leave you the nastiest comments. And it hurts. You will have to get to a place where it doesn't hurt you as much, if at all, but that resilience is learned over time. That's not natural to most people. People are wired to want to fit in.

Bhasin said it helps to remember that people only show the best parts of their lives on social media. People don't know you, truly, and when that's the case, it's easier to judge.

HEALTHY HABIT #4: SET PERSONAL BOUNDARIES

Set boundaries. Decide what you are comfortable sharing. Being an influencer is about authenticity, but people don't need oversharing, and you don't need it either. Decide ahead of time what you want to share with people. You always hold the power. If you don't want to share a part of yourself with people, that is okay. You have that right.

I respect influencers who keep their relationships private. That's cool. They do not allow everyone's opinions, praises, or adverse comments to get into this thing you're trying to build with another human being in real life.

In any case, have healthy relationships with your followers. They are fans to a degree. They don't honestly know you. Remember this. I've seen influencers start to relate to followers as friends because they DM each other often and have become super tight. Yes, there is space for that and it's an amazing opportunity social media can create. However, true friendship is a relationship. Unless they've met you or spent time with you, live over Zoom or in person, they are acquaintance-fans to many degrees because they really only know the version of you online. They're not doing real life with you.

Every emotion does not need to be shared on social media. It's super unhealthy and another reason why having a niche is so important. Stick to your topic and talk with yourself about what your posts will be and not be.

LIVING LIFE OUT LOUD AND ONLINE

People will always be there to judge you. It's inevitable. Don't fuel their flame with gasoline. Be mindful of what comments you leave online, what opinions you post, what video content you create. Always take a second to reevaluate if a message is important enough to post. If others are in the video or associated with the production, ask yourself, does it paint them positively? Are the people involved in the production reflective of your current values? Are you willing to accept the consequences, whether good or bad, that come with posting this content? Sit on it for a few hours if you need to. Do you still feel good about your decision to post? A few hours of thought will not cost you your career or clout, but it just might save it.

As an influencer, you are a public figure. You can get canceled at any time, so don't get cocky. I've worked in this industry long enough to see the rise and fall of many greats. Do you know why companies sell for hundreds of millions of dollars? It generally has very little to do with the company that can be duplicated. What makes a business valuable is its current customer and market data and its potential to capture even more.

Have a therapist you see regularly. Everyone needs support, an outside professional perspective. These days there are numerous affordable online therapy providers out there and many with free trials. Use them. Find your support system and constantly remind yourself who you are and why you do what you do. You are great, and online trolls are simply sad people who are struggling with their lives. Let no one's loud opinion ever alter how beautifully gifted or intelligent you are on your own. You define you. No one else. And remember you are on Instagram to provide a service and to get paid, sign checks, make friends, and then sign out.

So keep your business head on straight, be integrous, and take care of yourself first and foremost.

DO THIS NOW:
- Do you have structure in place to stay mentally well as an influencer? Make sure you practice thinking abundantly, taking time off, learning empathy and how to shift perspective, and setting personal boundaries for what you will share and not share.
- Do you have a strong support system outside of social

media? What do you need to do to get the support you need from a community that has your back? Join the Built to Influence community to connect with more influencers at built2influence.com.

- Get a therapist you can talk to whenever you need support. Find someone in your area or use Google to search "virtual therapy platforms" for the most cost-effective options.
- Go to brandpartnershipbible.com for additional micro influencer resources.

CONCLUSION

You've now read this book cover to cover. Yay, you! *Seriously.* But while insights are powerful, action is what gets you results and sustains success.

Deploy the strategies you learned if you haven't already, and reach out to me anytime at @_ashleighwarren because I want to hear from you. And since I know you're going to get in action immediately, I'll keep this final message short:

There is nothing you cannot do if you are willing to put patience and practice into it. Nothing. If you want a life of freedom, it's yours.

So, I'll see you on social. Or, hopefully in person in the near future. I can't wait to experience your content and the virtual world you create, and learn as a member of *your* community.

And please remember you're not alone in this; join the Built to Influence community anytime to become part of a network of thriving influencers who are living their dreams while expressing themselves online, having fun, earning serious coin, and making this world a better place.

The best is yet to come for you.

—Ash

ACKNOWLEDGMENTS

To my younger siblings, you are forever my inspiration. I am so proud of the humans you are becoming. I love you endlessly.

To my friends and chosen family, you have carried me over the years in ways that I can never thoroughly explain. There are not enough words. Thank you for your love and continuous support.

To my uncle Tony, I miss you. Thank you for always making me feel at home. I know you would have been one of the first to read this book front to back. I hope I have made you proud.

To my clients and team, none of this would have been possible without you. I appreciate your trust, creativity, and drive to continuously do cool shit with me.

Last but not least, I thank God for allowing me to live such a beautiful life filled with so many incredible people and experiences. Thank you for giving me purpose. Thank you for bringing me such amazing people. I owe it all to you.

BIBLIOGRAPHY

CHAPTER 1

Elise Dopson, "30+ Influencer Marketing Statistics to Have on Your Radar (2021)," shopify, August 18, 2021, https://www.shopify.com/blog/influencer-marketing-statistics.

"Collabstr Releases 2022 Influencer Marketing Report With Key Sector Data," GlobeNewsWire, December 7, 2021, https://www.globenewswire.com/news-release/2021/12/07/2347692/0/en/Collabstr-Releases-2022-Influencer-Marketing-Report-With-Key-Sector-Data.html.

"How Many Americans Are Self-Employed in 2021?" Oberlo, accessed October 15, 2021, https://www.oberlo.ca/statistics/how-many-america.

Areti Vassou, "List of Instagram Banned Hashtags," May 14, 2019, Ideadeco, https://ideadeco.co/2019/05/14/list-of-instagram-banned-hashtags-updated-2021/.

Werner Geyser, "The State of Influencer Marketing 2020: Benchmark Report," Influencer Marketing Hub, accessed December 21, 2021, https://influencermarketinghub.com/influencer-marketing-benchmark-report-2020/ns-are-self-employed.

Jonas Sickler, "What is E-A-T and Why it's Important (Google, E-A-T, and SEO)," Terakeet, April 30, 2021,https://terakeet.com/blog/what-is-eat/.

"Study: Micro Influencers Generate 7X More Engagement on Instagram than Influencers With Larger Followings", MaretingDive, October 9, 2018, https://www.marketingdive.com/press-release/20181009-study-micro influencers-generate-7x-more-engagement-on-instagram-than-infl-1/.

CHAPTER 5

Gary Vaynerchuk, "The $1.80 Instagram Strategy to Grow Your Business or Brand," Gary Vaynerchuk, accessed October 15, 2021, https://www.garyvaynerchuk.com/ instagram-for-business-180-strategy-grow-business-brand/.

Jillian Warren, "The Ultimate Guide to Instagram Influencer Marketing," LaterBlog, November 8, 2020, https://later.com/blog/ instagram-influencer-marketing/.

CHAPTER 6

Michael Glover, "Word of Mouth Marketing in 2021: How to Create a Strategy for Social Media Buzz & Skyrocket Referral Sales," BigCommerce, accessed December 29, 2021, https://www.bigcommerce.com/blog/ word-of-mouth-marketing/#word-of-mouth-marketing-statistics.

Yuyu Chen, "84 Percent of Millennials Don't Trust Traditional Advertising," ClickZ, March 4, 2015, https://www.clickz. com/84-percent-of-millennials-dont-trust-traditional-advertising/27030/.

CHAPTER 9

Jenni Gritters, "How Instagram Takes a Toll on Influencers' Brains," *The Guardian*, January 8, 2019, https://www.theguardian.com/us-news/2019/ jan/08/instagram-influencers-psychology-social-media-anxiety.

Robert T. Muller, "Social Media Affects Influencers' Mental Health," *Psychology Today*, October 6, 2021, https://www.psychologytoday.com/us/blog/talking-about-trauma/202110/social-media-affects-influencers-mental-health.

"Social Media and Mental Health," HelpGuide, accessed November 19, 2021, https://www.helpguide.org/articles/mental-health/social-media-and-mental-health.htm.

Heather Leighton, "Influencers Admit That Instagram is Bad for Body Image, Mental Healthy, Study Shows," *Forbes*, December 13, 2019, https://www.forbes.com/sites/heatherleighton/2019/12/13/is-instagram-bad-for-your-mental-health-body-image/?sh=6cd50b1e1e55.

"The Social Dilemma: Social Media and Your Mental Health," McleanHospital.org, accessed November 19, 2021, https://www.mcleanhospital.org/essential/it-or-not-social-medias-affecting-your-mental-health.

CPSIA information can be obtained
at www.ICGtesting.com
Printed in the USA
LVHW041920200623
750234LV00001B/83